"This must-read book for fellowship advisors should be shared with their students. Lassonde's success with first-generation college students has produced a 'developmental' guide to writing the personal statement emphasizing applicant growth, rather than a singular focus on winning. No matter their starting line, no matter the outcome, your students will gain a sense of who they are, what they care about, articulate their goals, and hone their life's purpose."

Jonathan F. Fanton, *President Emeritus, American Academy of Arts and Sciences*

"I wish I'd had this book by my side throughout my three decades of advising students. Using clear language and illuminating examples, Lassonde draws a map for advisors to guide their students through what is often an opaque process, showing how the well-executed personal statement enables applicants to learn about themselves, and in so doing, become better versions of the people they hoped to be in the first place."

Jonathan Holloway, *President, Rutgers University*

"On my campus I advise many students who begin to think about applying for fellowships sometime during their college years. Stephen Lassonde's book is chock full of 'real world,' super low-cost methods for helping fellowship applicants from modest backgrounds. Faculty and staff at every university should use this book: 'a friendly read' and broadly applicable with so many concrete suggestions."

Richard J. Light, *Pforzheimer Professor of Teaching and Learning, Harvard University*

Helping Your Students Write Personal Statements

This practical book is a timely and comprehensive guide designed for college advisors and instructors who are supporting and coaching students into successful internships, fellowships, graduate programs, and professional schools. This book emphasizes the most important part of any application, the personal statement: how to prepare to write it, how to draft it, how to revise it—and why to invest time in the process of developing it. *Helping Your Students Write Personal Statements* analyzes the components of the effective personal statement and provides examples from many successful essays by actual college students, as well as exercises for students. It also gives advisors the tools to help engage students who might not ordinarily consider themselves credible candidates for nationally competitive fellowships. This book uniquely takes a developmental approach, offering college advisors and teachers a concrete, step-by-step plan to help any student craft the best, most persuasive personal statement they can write, helping transform their students into compelling, competitive candidates.

Stephen Lassonde is Director of the Newman Office of Prestigious Scholarships & Fellowships at Hunter College, City University of New York. He was formerly Dean of Student Life at Harvard College, Deputy Dean of the College at Brown University, and an Assistant Dean at Yale College. Lassonde has previously published on the history of childhood and education in the United States.

Helping Your Students Write Personal Statements

Framing the Narrative for Fellowships and Other Opportunities

Stephen Lassonde

NEW YORK AND LONDON

Designed cover image: Rachael Wakeford, Office of Communications, Hunter College, City University of New York

First published 2024
by Routledge
605 Third Avenue, New York, NY 10158

and by Routledge
4 Park Square, Milton Park, Abingdon, Oxon, OX14 4RN

Routledge is an imprint of the Taylor & Francis Group, an informa business

© 2024 Stephen Lassonde

The right of Stephen Lassonde to be identified as author of this work has been asserted in accordance with sections 77 and 78 of the Copyright, Designs and Patents Act 1988.

All rights reserved. No part of this book may be reprinted or reproduced or utilised in any form or by any electronic, mechanical, or other means, now known or hereafter invented, including photocopying and recording, or in any information storage or retrieval system, without permission in writing from the publishers.

Trademark notice: Product or corporate names may be trademarks or registered trademarks, and are used only for identification and explanation without intent to infringe.

ISBN: 978-1-032-59604-4 (hbk)
ISBN: 978-1-032-59558-0 (pbk)
ISBN: 978-1-003-45538-7 (ebk)

DOI: 10.4324/9781003455387

Typeset in Perpetua
by MPS Limited, Dehradun

To Margaret, who sees and celebrates the big picture even as she fixes its stray commas, errant hyphens, and misplaced modifiers.

Contents

Acknowledgements	x
Preface	xv

1 What Our Students Don't Know: What Is a Fellowship, and Why Apply for One? 1

2 Common Denominators: What It Takes to Be a Successful Applicant 19

3 "Who Are You?" Helping Your Students Know Who They Are 40

4 What a Fellowship Committee Wants to Know about Your Student: Helping Your Students Understand How to Present Themselves 58

5 Framing the Narrative: Authenticity in the Personal Statement 68

6 Where to Begin? Getting Your Students Started on Writing Their Personal Statements 84

7 Revising and Ending: Helping Your Students Understand the Importance of Refining Their Personal Statements 95

Conclusion: Recruiting, Cultivating, and Retaining Student Talent, and Faculty Collaboration 107

Index 116

Acknowledgements

"Prepare yourself to do the thing you aspire to but be ever open to the unknown satisfactions of unforeseen opportunity." This piece of advice is what thirty years of advising undergraduates has taught me. It is the thing I say whenever one of my students asks me if they are headed down the right path. It is the thing I say to myself whenever I am faced with change, serendipity, or apparent misfortune.

This book is a product of my accumulated learning, but it would never have come into being if Jennifer J. Raab, former President of Hunter College, hadn't recruited me to Hunter as I was leaving Harvard. Jennifer's commitment to Hunter's students inspired her to create a fellowships office and to persuade Hunter alumna Ruth Newman and her husband Harold, to endow it. As I've heard Jennifer say so many times, "We knew we had the talent here, we just needed someone to organize it." It has been my privilege and pleasure to organize that talent each year since the fall of 2016, and I thank Jennifer for trusting me to make the most of the opportunity. Thanks to the Newmans' foresight and generosity, this guidance will continue long past my tenure. I have Dr. Harold Koplewicz to thank for introducing me to Jennifer. He has since become a great friend and mentor in all things. I was introduced to Harold by my dear friend and three-time co-teacher, Dr. Ruth Westheimer, to whom I also owe much.

Mentoring is a major theme of this book, and so I want to acknowledge my own mentors extending back to my years in college. Each of them has been crucial in some way to my professional or intellectual development and several of them remain in my life and are the people I turn to when I have an important decision to make, or news to share. They are, in chronological order: Chuck Chalberg, John Modell, Lary May, Elaine Tyler May, Jon Butler, John Demos, Joe Gordon, Richard Brodhead, Edith N. MacMullen, William Kessen, Paula Fass, William Sledge, Betsy Sledge, Jonathan Holloway, Steven Mintz, Katherine Bergeron, Michael Ignatieff, and Judith Friedlander. Thomas

ACKNOWLEDGEMENTS

("Dodie") McDow's wisdom, humor, and insight into the human condition have sustained me through the ups and downs of life for the past twenty years. Karilyn Crockett's professional perspective and personal generosity have saved me from numerous pitfalls as I navigated my way through this book. Both, though much younger than I, have joined the ranks of my more senior, long-coveted mentors.

My journey into the world of formal fellowship advising began as I was departing Cambridge. And so, my formal thank-you's include my former colleagues in the Harvard College Dean's Office, preeminently, Dean of Freshmen Tom Dingman, Gene Corbin, and Allston Burr Resident Deans Adam Muri-Rosenthal, Luke Leafgren, Michael Canfield, Bilal Malik, and Laura Johnson. Greg Llacer, (roughly) my counterpart at Harvard and a good colleague, became a selfless source of support and advice as I joined this calling. He has been of critical help as I drafted and redrafted this book, and I owe him very special thanks. Asad Asad, Resident Tutor and Fellowships Coordinator at Mather House when I lived there, offered sound advice before I embarked on my new career, as did then-recent Rhodes winner Hassaan Shahawy. Faculty Deans Christie McDonald and Michael Rosengarten were both gracious hosts and steadfast friends during and after my time at Mather House. Words cannot express my gratitude for their support. Michael Ignatieff and Zsuzsanna Zsohar, similarly, were staunch advocates and treasured neighbors at Mather who immediately became irreplaceable, lifelong friends.

Awaiting me at Hunter when I arrived were two incomparable colleagues, Judith Friedlander, who served as Dean of Arts and Sciences (and the year before I arrived, part-time fellowships advisor) and Lev Sviridov, Director of the Macaulay Honors College at Hunter. Lev, too, numbers among my "junior mentors," and I have benefitted mightily from his expertise in cultivating and preparing Hunter's Rhodes and Marshall candidates. Myrna Fader capably coordinated the Fulbright, Beinecke, and Jeannette K. Watson scholarships at Hunter before I arrived and during my first few years here. Jennie LaMonte and Andrew Klaber offered generous counsel in my early years, as I got my bearings.

I've benefitted from a string of benevolent supervisors at Hunter, past and present: Lon Kaufman, Eija Ayravainen, Bill Tramontano, Steve Mintz, and particularly Daniel Hurewitz, whose imagination and care continually challenge me to do my job better. I have also prospered with the aid of colleagues in the President's, Provost's and Deans' offices, extending back to my first days at Hunter: Christa Acampora, Niki Bennett, Theresa Bradley, Chris Braun, Brian Buckwald, Livia Cangemi, Rob Cowan, Farjana Kabir, Sean Kenealy, Cynthia Vance King, Geralyn Lederman, Anne Lytle, Lori Mazor, Kevin Nesbitt, Manoj Pardasani, Andy Polsky, Nelson Restrepo, John Rose, Malkie Schwartz, and Miesha Smith. Also, I want to thank Eve Levy in Advancement, Michael

ACKNOWLEDGEMENTS

Middleton, Jennifer Tuten, Matthew Caballero, Jade Young Michaels, Jason Riffaterre in the School of Education, and Vince DiMiceli, Devin Callahan, Eve Jacobson Kessler, and Rachael Wakeford in Communications.

I have been surrounded by unusually talented colleagues in Hunter's Pre-Professional Advising Center. Elise Jaffe has been a special collaborator and we are surrounded by the support of many others: Nina Ledis Cannon, Elise Harris, Kemile Jackson, Naomi Press, and Peggy Segal, as well as Krysta Battersby, Sarah Craver, Emma Heineman, Gabriella Vetrano, and Alyssa Wheeler. Cris Gleicher has been essential to the selection of Jeannette K. Watson nominees each year. Marlene Hennessy, Catherine Coppola, Jason Young, and Sarah Jeninsky of the Thomas Hunter Honors Program annually send their most promising students in my direction, as have Vasiliy Arkanov and Elizabeth Wall-O'Brien. Kelvin Black, Hunter's Director of the Mellon Mays Undergraduate Fellowship, has served on numerous fellowship selection committees with me and is an astute source of advice and insight.

The faculty at Hunter have been generous and enthusiastic in their support of my efforts but, more importantly, wonderful mentors and teachers to our students: I have benefitted in particular from the help of Manu Bhagavan, Philip Alcabes, Linda Alcoff, Amber Alliger, Ronnie Ancona, Lisa Anderson, Nebahat Avcıoğlu, Andrea Baden, Laura Baecher, Jill Bargonetti, Susan Barile, Rick Belsky, Jacqueline Brown, Lynn Chancer, Der-lin Chao, Wen-Shing Chou, Susanna Cole, Rebecca Connor, Kelle Cruz, Partha Deb, Laurel Eckhardt, Alexander Elison, Leonard Feldman, Nancy Foner, Allan Frei, Scott Gentile, Jeremy Glick, Janette Gomos Klein, Nancy Greenbaum, Stephen Greenbaum, Owen Gutfreund, D'Weston Haywood, Benjamin Hett, Mandë Holford, Harold Holzer, Bingying Hu, Nico Israel, Alexis Jemal, Robert Jenkins, Victoria Johnson, Richard Kaye, Yasha Klots, Robert Koehl, Michael Lee, Dorchen Leidholdt, Vivian Louie, Daniel Mailick, Robyn Marasco, Erin Mayo-Adam, Elidor Mëhilli, Janet Neary, Jessica Neuwirth, Elke Nicolai, Kelly Nims, Sonali Perera, David Petrain, Jody Polleck, Shirley Raps, Mary Roldán, Jonathan Rosenberg, Jessica Rothman, Laura Schor, Sanford Schram, Zachary Shirkey, Basil Smikle, William Solecki, Carolyn Somerville, Barbara Sproul, Michael Steiper, Christopher Stone, Charles Tien, and Shyama Venkateswar.

Since arriving in New York, I've had the great fortune of being able to consult with some of the most knowledgeable fellowship professionals in the nation: Michelle Douenias, Sarah Fischer, Diane Flynn, Rob Garris, Craig Harwood, Chris Kasabach, Ling Li, Sara Nolfo, Andrew Rich, and Mariko Silver.

A number of friends, professional associates, and former students have offered the benefit of their expertise and experience, often at a moment's notice. I've called upon each of them to advise students or to help prepare them for interviews: Jacob Cannon, David Denby, Linda Dunleavy, Cynthia Farrar, Paul Gottlieb, Janet Halley, Tad Heuer, Andrew Intelkofer, Josh Jelly-Shapiro, Paul

ACKNOWLEDGEMENTS

Kennedy, Aaron Kennon, David Lawrence, Laura Liberman, Joel Rosenthal, Alex Roth, Amia Srinivasan, Susan Steinhardt, Paul Urayama, and Tina Wu.

Several trusted colleagues generously read all or parts of the manuscript at various stages of development: Karilyn Crockett, John Demos, Michelle Douenias, Jonathan Fanton, Judith Friedlander, Craig Harwood, Jonathan Holloway, Daniel Hurewitz, Chris Kasabach, Richard J. Light, Dodie McDow, and Susan Rieger. Special thanks to Steve Mintz, who offered a most encouraging review of the manuscript after I had redrafted it.

My warm thanks to Rosemary Deen for granting me permission to a reproduce portions of her published work in this book. The work of Richard J. Light, Agnes Callard, and William Damon has inspired my overall philosophy of advising and helped me to think effectively about fellowship advising in particular. Robert Steven Kaplan's essay on self-awareness through autobiography has become an important guide in teaching my students about self-understanding through narrative.

I've been blessed with legions of talented students at each of the schools I've worked at. I want to acknowledge those I taught or advised: Sam Koplewicz at Brown and at Harvard, Dianisbeth Acquie, Brett Biebelberg, Greg Briker, Marlee Ehrlich, Will Holub-Moorman, Margaret Irving, Ivan Levingston, Hassaan Shahawy, Joule Voelz, Langston Ward, and Katie Wu. At Hunter I've learned as much about fellowship advising from the hundreds of students I've worked with as I have taught them about applying for fellowships. While I am indebted to all of them, the following students deserve my special thanks for having shared their time and perspectives in my writing workshops and for helping their fellow students with mock interviews: Madelyn Adams, Nibras Ahmed, Malik Atajanow, Gabriella Cook-Francis, Elliot David, Victoria DiTomasso, Izzy Gouse, Calvin Herman, Tom Hutton, Thamara Jean, Nicole Krishtul, Matthew LoCastro, Chloé Lee, Hannah Lynch, Faiza Masood, Michael Mazzeo, Cloé Mueller, Ilanith Nizard, Joy Nuga, Cerimar Olivares, Swara Patel, Juliana Poroye, Andrew Shkreli, Priya Singh, Jessica Sirico, Christina Valeros, and Saif Zihiri. The following students graciously allowed me to reproduce parts of their essays, photographs, and other teaching materials in this book: Devashish Basnet, Gerson Borrero, Daniel Hickey, Emily Johnson, Hassaan Shahawy, Alice Tsai, Maisha Uddin, and Anna Vera. Very special thanks to Demi Moore, who has contributed to this book in so many ways and is one of those students who brings out the best in her teachers and advisors.

I would like to thank my agents at Inkwell Management, Michael Carlisle and Michael Mungiello, who gave me crucial support throughout the process of drafting the manuscript and finding a publisher. At Routledge, Heather Jarrow, Marielena Zajac, Helen Strain, Simon Jacobs, and Tom Bedford were more generous and patient than I deserved, and I wouldn't have completed it without their enthusiastic backing.

ACKNOWLEDGEMENTS

Finally, a number of close friends have been hearing about my work at Hunter and specifically about this book for the past few years. I am indebted to them in so many ways and look forward to repaying them in the years to come for their indulgence: Ann Gaylin and Michael Flynt have offered succor and a home away from home. Carol Cohen, Albrecht Funk, Joe Gordon, Karen Krahulik, Dodie McDow, John Modell, Adam Muri-Rosenthal, Celeste Palmero, Judith Schachter, Linda Sirow, and Paul Strickland have been indispensable touchstones. My older son, Alex Lassonde, his brother Jonathan Lassonde, Jonathan's wife, Allyson Schumacher, and their son Theo are an abiding source of pride and affection.

This book had its origins in the magical workshop that Margaret Sabin and I created and developed during our first year at Hunter. This incubator of student talent has "graduated" more than 350 students, 80% of whom subsequently won a fellowship or were admitted to a top graduate, law, or medical school. Margaret not only gets us through the minutiae of the business end of life but fills each day with conversation, inspiration, beauty, mirth, and grace. Margaret makes me a better father, brother, friend, and colleague, thus, my most profound thanks go to her—loving companion in everything.

Preface

Fellowship advisors inhabit an important role at a pivotal moment. With growing recognition of the need to diversify candidate pools by fellowship-granting organizations of every kind, fellowship advisors have both the ability and the responsibility to bring forward students who can lead this transformation.[1] But identifying potential candidates is only the first step toward increasing the tremendous variety of candidate talent, nationally. Because the inherent exclusivity of nationally competitive fellowships in many ways epitomizes "the hidden curriculum," when inexperienced students wade into the application cycle, they're often unaware of everything entailed.[2] So, one of our most important jobs is to initiate the uninitiated.

Part of this initiation is to help our students appreciate that the application *process* presents an invaluable opportunity for them to contemplate their college experience, personal philosophy, values, goals, and future plans. At the heart of this process is the personal statement, both because it creates time and space for critical introspection and because it is so important to an application's success. However, the time and energy our students expend applying for fellowships exists in tension, often, with their motive for applying, which is to be rewarded for their efforts with a scholarship. One of our goals as "guides" to our students, then, is to help them resolve this tension so that the process of applying surpasses the outcome in the long run.[3]

Paradoxically, despite its centrality to the application process, the personal statement remains its least understood component. Most advice about writing the personal statement pertains to specific scholarships (Rhodes, Marshall, etc.) in a "how-to" format, scattered across the internet and designed to be consumed "on-demand." This book, contrarily, takes a developmental approach to fellowship personal statements—how to bring together all the ingredients that go into the personal statement; organize self-reflection; and manage the balance of form and content in what is a singularly unfamiliar form of writing.[4]

I wrote this book for my colleagues—professionals like me who advise college students applying for fellowships and scholarships at the national level. Some of

PREFACE

you are faculty members at small liberal arts colleges who serve in this capacity part-time in exchange for course relief. Others of you are directors of honors programs who assist scholarship applicants in the course of supporting your institution's most promising undergraduates. Many of the rest of us are part-time or full-time fellowship advisors, from "one-person-shops" to directors of offices with several specialist staff members. And I can conceive of two other users of this book: those of you who are faculty at small liberal arts colleges that have a good number of talented students but no fellowships office to guide them systematically, and teachers at community colleges whose students distinguish themselves through their drive and intellectual curiosity but need direction and support not available, typically, until they reach a four-year college.

I want to make clear at the outset that I am a relative newcomer to this field. In fact, you may rightly see me as an interloper in a calling you've been practicing successfully for many years already. My familiarity with you as peers has been gleaned mostly through the discussion threads and email queries on the National Association of Fellowship Advisors listserv and through the extended "conversations" that have weaved their way through the series of excellent books reproducing NAFA's conference proceedings initiated early in the organization's existence by Suzanne McCray. The wisdom shared through these many conversations, both by foundation professionals and fellowship advisors, has been extremely useful to me as I've felt my way through the process of setting up a fellowships office at Hunter College. From these ongoing discussions I've learned what foundations seek in successful candidates and how we as advisors can encourage and support potential applicants. Valuable, too, are the important philosophical/ethical issues that arise in so many of the essays collected in the volumes edited by McCray et al., both in the advising we provide and the ways our students apply it.

Part of my motive, however, in writing this book has been to offer the view of someone still new to this enterprise in hopes that a novel perspective would be both helpful and welcomed by others, especially those just starting out. Moreover, I came to realize early while toiling in this field that virtually everyone who advises fellowship applicants comes from somewhere else. Our "training" is eclectic. Most of us, it seems, just "fell into" this work and I'm only sorry it took me so long to understand that this work is what I was meant to do. So, if at first you take me for an interloper, I hope you will soon come to see me as a fellow traveler who, like you, finds that the most satisfying part of my job is learning just *who* is sitting across from me when a student finds their way to my office to talk about applying for a scholarship.

Three of this book's chapters are perhaps most useful for experienced advisors and for faculty at smaller institutions: Chapter 2, "Common Denominators: What It Takes to Be a Successful Applicant"; Chapter 5, "Framing the Narrative: Authenticity in the Personal Statement"; and the

Conclusion, "Recruiting, Cultivating, and Retaining Student Talent, and Faculty Collaboration." Chapters 2 and 5 discuss the qualities and attributes found in potential scholarship candidates and how your students can write personal statements that will provide a future template for their fellowship or graduate and professional school applications. The Conclusion suggests that the recent interest in diversifying our fellowship applicant pools has presented an opportunity to think about the work we do as a branch of liberal education with the potential to serve all of our students. And there I discuss recruitment practices to engage students of every kind.

If each of us has come to this work from somewhere else, what we have in common is that every one of us has had a teacher who took an interest in us because we showed special promise. You wouldn't have gotten where you are professionally without the guidance your teachers offered simply because you loved their subjects; and in turn, your engagement with students who stick out from the crowd is one of the most rewarding aspects of advising scholarship applicants. Like the mentoring that faculty perform to repay the moral debt they carry forward from having been mentored themselves, your stewardship of students in the fellowship application process can be life-changing for your students. My hope is that this book will help you guide your students in the new world of fellowships that has blossomed since you were an undergraduate.

I don't presume to have specialized knowledge and I'm certainly less familiar with the details and nuances of particular fellowships than many of you. What I have to offer is experience at three highly selective institutions as an all-around academic advisor. My engagement with undergraduates has been extensive and deep. I've had the privilege of witnessing the unfolding of thousands of young people's lives on the precipice of their adulthood until my own professional unfolding landed me here at Hunter College in my current role as fellowships advisor. I came to my present position at a unique juncture in the history of fellowship award-making, just as the organizations that fund major national fellowship programs were beginning to recognize the need to diversify their candidate pools as well as their fellowship winners.

Most of the students at my university are some combination of first-generation college students with high financial need, students of color, and immigrants, or the children of immigrants. Most work at half-time jobs, have significant family obligations, and commute to campus each day. Even more than most post-secondary students these days, a significant ratio of students at my university arrive seeking a degree that will enable them to go into a profession related to healthcare.[5] The vast majority of them are from in-state and most come from one of New York City's five boroughs or Long Island. Almost without exception, they are determined to get their degrees without being deterred by anything but the most necessary deviation (like a job) because their parents worry about their distraction from the straight line between college and careers they know: medicine, law, engineering, or business. Unsure what a "fellowship" is, most of our students don't take the time to find out, think it doesn't pertain to them, or assume that, like studying abroad, it may require an investment of time and energy with uncertain benefits.

If you are at an institution like mine, you know exactly what I'm talking about. If you're not, you may have more limited encounters with the kinds of students I have described here. But this book, I hope, will be helpful to advisors at both ends of the spectrum of higher education. If you are, again, at a campus like mine, you are probably understaffed, serve hundreds of students and may not have the time to raise your head long enough to see the bigger picture—all the obstacles our students commonly face that either discourage them from applying or sap their will to complete started applications. The external obstacles are apparent because our students are more likely to identify and verbalize them. The "internal" obstacles are, by definition, invisible and borne by our students in silence and isolation. Imposter syndrome is the most common by-product of our students' belief that they cannot contend for nationally competitive scholarships—and so wouldn't even dream of dreaming about applying for them. Financial pressures, family pressures, and a utilitarian/vocational attitude toward their education pose other unseen obstacles. And of course, the most insidious is their inability to conceive of how to cultivate all-important relationships with potential mentors. Our challenge then at big, public universities is to identify, cultivate, and support students who often lack the confidence and knowledge to compete for fellowships.

If, however, you are a fellowships advisor at a highly selective, resource-rich college, your first-generation, immigrant, and (many) students of color are, nonetheless, subject to the same factors that discourage their peers nationwide from applying for fellowships.[6] Your challenge, contrariwise, is that you have your hands full with students who readily self-identify as candidates for the most sought-after opportunities. You may, therefore, be less engaged with students reluctant to push themselves forward to apply for these awards, simply because you're overwhelmed by the demands of organizing the surfeit of talent at your institution. My hope is that you may find some of the observations that follow helpful in cultivating students for fellowships who need more direct encouragement than the average fellowship applicant on your campus.

My observations in this book are based on my experience as an advisor on campuses that take a "whole student" approach to guiding their students' development, which I think optimizes advising, whatever the context. In other words, my perspective here is student-focused rather than fellowship-focused. A significant part of what I have to offer my students I learned in my previous positions about the specific forms of support that highly selective colleges are able to provide their fellowship applicants—support I knew was effective and could be applied at low cost with high impact in my new setting. I did so immediately (with no small amount of good luck) and immediate results. The other portion I learned from my students—in my previous jobs, to be sure, but especially in my current position at Hunter College, which is a member of one the most diverse public urban universities in the United States. And just as I remind my students, win or not, luck plays a role in the outcome of every fellowship they will apply for; my students' success *writ large* has to do in part with the fortuitousness of good timing as well. Were fellowship-granting foundations not, during the last decade, increasingly alive to the desirability of seeking variety in their applicant pools, even my most worthy and talented students might not have had the success they currently enjoy.

Good advising of any kind is based on one's ability to gain the trust of one's students. For me, trust is the key to unlocking student potential in the realm of fellowships as well. It's not just "buy-in" you seek, in the sense of wanting your students to recognize that you have something important to offer them. It's building the kind of relationships that Richard Light describes so well in *Making the Most of College*, where he discusses the most optimal, nurturing kind of relations between students and their mentors.[7] True mentoring takes time to germinate, bloom, and culminate in the kind of trust that allows you to be candid with your students about the quality of their work, so that they will believe you as readily when you tell them their essays "sing" as when you tell them they need more work. Securing their trust makes it possible for you to help them believe in themselves as they learn how to tell their own stories in the context of what they hope to accomplish intellectually and professionally.

*

A few words about myself, because who I am informs the way I see my students and what I have to offer them but also because I recognize that each of us in this field has something unique to bring to the work we do with our students. I read recently that, nationally, more than half of current tenure-track faculty have at least one parent with a graduate degree and "that faculty are up to 25 times more likely [than the general population] to have a parent with a Ph.D."[8] I vividly recall how cowed I was in graduate school (initially) by classmates who seemed most at ease and in command among our peers in seminar. They were at an entirely different level in their ability to confidently assert their opinions about our readings. Among our classmates, they seemed most certain about where they were headed and that they deserved to succeed. Most of them, I remember learning at the time, had parents who were professors or who at the very least held advanced academic degrees.

I started my post-secondary education in a suburban community college in Minnesota in the late 1970s. (More about this later.) I advanced to the University of Minnesota's flagship campus and completed a BA there in history. Later I had the good fortune of getting into a PhD program at Yale, where I had wonderful professors and a first-rate education. While I published my

PREFACE

dissertation and continue to conduct research and publish in my field, I wound up using my degree to secure a position as an academic advisor during the prolonged depressed job market in the humanities. I have no regrets. Each of the jobs I've had in academic advising, I have loved.

Unlike so many of my students here at Hunter, I'm not the child of immigrants and I'm not a person of color. But my parents were barely a generation removed from the working class, and I developed an understanding of what my students were experiencing psychologically, at each of the places I worked. As I explain later in this book, completing college was not a foregone conclusion in my household. Fewer than 40% of my graduating class in the public high school I attended applied to college, my father had attended college at night school while he was in the military, and my mother finished her interrupted college education by returning to school with me when I entered community college. I didn't have the kind of cultural capital that would have predicted success. I didn't understand the things I needed to about how to conduct myself in college and how to be successful afterward. But I had the good fortune of having teachers who took an interest in me and helped me flourish. In other words, through experience, I acquired both the imagination and empathy sufficient to comprehend what my students did and did not know, how to listen to them, and to resist the temptation to tell them what was "right" for them. Most important, I learned how to build trust with them. This is who I am and if I am to engender your trust as a reader and a colleague, know that I share with you the enormous satisfaction that comes from a job that helps the students we work with fulfill their dreams and the dreams of their families. I hope that some of the wisdom contained here is useful to you, that you will share some of the insights you find here with your students, or even better, recommend this book to them to read for themselves.

As I began teaching students how to write the personal statement for the first time, I was forced to reflect concretely and systematically on the essential elements of the essay, what worked and why. Having composed my first personal statement as a sophomore in college for an NEH grant program that no longer exists, I learned a skill that became fundamental to my survival when I attended graduate school, at a time when stipendiary support for graduate study beyond what one could earn as a teaching assistant was a rarity. When I began graduate school, moreover, I already had one child and would have another by the time I took my oral exam to enter candidacy for the PhD. I was literally supporting my family on my earnings as a teaching fellow and credit cards. I *had* to become proficient at applying for support outside my university if I was going to complete my degree. Fortunately, I was able to win a couple of major research fellowships and some smaller ones as well to get across the finish line. Once I began teaching and deaning, over the course of many years I found myself regularly in the orbit of the fellowship application process: as I read my students' fellowship personal statements and participated in my colleges' mock interview committees, I also served on a wide range of internal fellowship committees at each of my universities, and at Yale, was tasked with writing the nominating letters for my students who were candidates for the Rhodes, Marshall, Luce, and other national scholarships. In the process, I acquired a keen, if still intuitive, experiential sense of what went into an effective personal statement.

As is the case with any form of teaching, once I became responsible for explaining the elements and process of writing the personal statement, I had to understand it as a form of writing, for myself, first. This book in good part is the product of that effort, as well as the personal statement writing workshop that Margaret Sabin co-developed and has taught with me for the past several years at Hunter. Because it's impossible to know what one's colleagues do or do not know, will or won't find helpful (because our experience as fellowship advisors varies so widely), I've written this book assuming my reader has basic but not deep background in scholarship advising, striving to be as inclusive as possible in the advice that follows. My ideal reader is someone who cares about their students' success and understands the centrality of the personal statement to their students' personal, intellectual, and professional development. At the same time, however, I hope my "delivery" doesn't distance our more experienced colleagues who may feel in skimming this work that the territory I cover here is so familiar that they've nothing to gain from it.

Chapter 5 distills what I understood after I stood back and looked hard at what worked and what didn't. So, for those of you who have been advising students for many years, I hope you are curious enough to read this chapter to see if what I say resonates with your own observations and whether you have come to the some of the same conclusions about writing the personal statement. If nothing else, I hope that what I have to say commits to print the kind of wisdom you yourself have accrued over the years and have bestowed on your own students "in the moment" but which can now be shared in a more systematic, formal fashion. For those of you who are somewhat new to fellowship advising, the book as a whole tries to make explicit and in linear fashion, all the dimensions of your students' experiences that play a role in who they are as applicants, how to make sense of themselves, and how they can begin composing their own narratives. This will be useful to them regardless of whether they succeed in applying for fellowships or not, because the stories they tell about themselves will be crucial as they apply for internships, jobs, or admission to graduate school.

Two final notes before we begin. First, and I will repeat this elsewhere because it's important: your student's personal story, no matter how compelling, is secondary to the project they want to carry out and their explanation for needing the fellowship to see it through. This must be central

PREFACE

to the application; and my assumption is that in working with their mentors your students will have demonstrated their ability to formulate scholarly questions and have a sense of how to answer them. This is why I largely don't address this aspect of your students' applications. And second, while this book is addressed to you as advisors, most chapters include exercises intended for your students, to assist them in the process of collecting, arranging, and reflecting upon the elements of their personal statements before they sit down to draft them.

NOTES

1. The desirability of diversifying the candidate pools of nationally competitive scholarships was articulated at an international conference on the goals, purpose, and practice of candidate selection held at Bellagio, Italy, in 2002. See Alice Stone Ilchman, Warren F. Ilchman, and Mary Hale Tolar, "Strengthening Nationally Competitive Scholarships: An Overview," chap. 1 in *The Lucky Few and the Worthy Many: Scholarship Competitions and the World's Future Leaders*, ed. Alice Stone Ilchman, Warren F. Ilchman, and Mary Hale Tolar (Bloomington, IN: Indiana University Press, 2004). This issue was raised again soon after the establishment of the National Association of Fellowships Advisors (NAFA) and was the organizing theme at NAFA's 2011 biennial conference. Indeed, a number of essays published from that conference's proceedings underscored this message while stressing the importance of the relationship between scholarship advising and liberal learning. To cite just two examples, see William Gates, Sr., "Democratizing the World of Scholarships," chap. 1, and Elizabeth Vardaman, "Recalculating: A Sojourn Down Scholarship Road to the Deep Heart's Core," chap. 8, in *All In: Expanding Access Through Nationally Competitive Awards*, ed. Suzanne McCray (Fayetteville, AK: University of Arkansas Press, 2013). Fellowship foundations took up this mission in earnest beginning in 2020 when the Rhodes Trust noted that one of its goals in five key action areas was to "Widen and Diversify the Distribution of Rhodes Scholarships." See "Legacy, Equity, & Inclusion" on the website of the Rhodes Trust, www.rhodeshouse.ox.ac.uk/impact-legacy/legacy-equity-inclusion/. Other major scholarships have similarly taken up this cause.
2. Rachel Gable, *The Hidden Curriculum: First Generation Students at Legacy Universities* (Princeton, NJ: Princeton University Press, 2021).
3. On this point, I benefitted particularly from the discussion in Richelle Bernazzoli, Joanna Dickert, Anne Moore, and Jason Kelly Roberts, "Excellent Sheep or Passionate Weirdos? Fellowships and Fellowships Advising as Vehicles for Self-Authorship," in *Bridging the Gap: Perspectives on Nationally Competitive Scholarships*, ed. Suzanne McCray and Dana Kuchem (Fayetteville, AK: University of Arkansas Press, 2019), 43–64.
4. From the very founding of the National Association of Fellowship Advisors to the present, practitioners have stressed the importance of the *process* of applying for fellowships as the most important reward for applicants. See Suzanne McCray, Introduction to *Beyond Winning: National Scholarship Competitions and the Student Experience*, ed. Suzanne McCray (Fayetteville, AK: University of Arkansas Press, 2005), xi.

5. In 2022, 38% of Hunter's students indicated at the point of enrollment that they intended to major in a course of study related to health or science, according to Joseph Fantozzi, Jr., Senior Director of Admissions at Hunter College.
6. It's important here to qualify the overbroad phrase "students of color" because, as Anthony Jack details, even among Black college students, there exists a wide range of differences in terms of the relationship between educational legacy and cultural and social capital. See Anthony Abraham Jack, *The Privileged Poor: How Elite Colleges Are Failing Disadvantaged Students* (Cambridge, MA: Harvard University Press, 2019).
7. Richard J. Light, *Making the Most Out of College: Students Speak Their Minds* (Cambridge, MA: Harvard University Press, 2001).
8. Michael T. Nietzel, "The Well-Heeled Professoriate: Socioeconomic Backgrounds of University Faculty," *Forbes*, March 28, 2021, www.forbes.com/sites/michaeltnietzel/2021/03/28/the-well-heeled-professoriate-socioeconomic-backgrounds-of-university-faculty/?sh=1efc329c5e22. Nietzel's article is based on findings reported in Allison C. Morgan et al., "Socioeconomic Roots of Academic Faculty," *Nature Human Behaviour* 6 (August 29, 2022): 1625–33, https://doi.org/10.1038/s41562-022-01425-4.
9. Memorably, a Yale Graduate School administrator once said to me that it was actually a *good* thing that graduate students needed to be entrepreneurial in financing their education because it prepared them to become successful grant-getters as future faculty members. Despite how tone-deaf this sounded to me at the time, it turns out he was right: I was driven by my desperation to become good at applying for fellowships.

WORKS CITED

Bernazzoli, Richelle, Joanna Dickert, Anne Moore, and Jason Kelly Roberts. "Excellent Sheep or Passionate Weirdos? Fellowships and Fellowships Advising as Vehicles for Self-Authorship." In *Bridging the Gap: Perspectives on Nationally Competitive Scholarships*, edited by Suzanne McCray and Dana Kuchem. Fayetteville, AK: University of Arkansas Press, 2019.

Gable, Rachel. *The Hidden Curriculum: First Generation Students at Legacy Universities.* Princeton, NJ: Princeton University Press, 2021.

Gates, Sr., William. "Democratizing the World of Scholarships." In *All In: Expanding Access Through Nationally Competitive Awards*, edited by Suzanne McCray. Fayetteville, AK: University of Arkansas Press, 2013.

Ilchman, Alice Stone, Warren F. Ilchman, and Mary Hale Tolar. "Strengthening Nationally Competitive Scholarships: An Overview." In *The Lucky Few and the Worthy Many: Scholarship Competitions and the World's Future Leaders*, edited by Alice Stone Ilchman, Warren F. Ilchman, and Mary Hale Tolar. Bloomington, IN: Indiana University Press, 2004.

Jack, Anthony Abraham. *The Privileged Poor: How Elite Colleges Are Failing Disadvantaged Students.* Cambridge, MA: Harvard University Press, 2019.

Light, Richard J. *Making the Most Out of College: Students Speak Their Minds.* Cambridge, MA: Harvard University Press, 2001.

PREFACE

McCray, Suzanne. Introduction to *Beyond Winning: National Scholarship Competitions and the Student Experience*, edited by Suzanne McCray. Fayetteville, AK: University of Arkansas Press, 2005.

Morgan, Allison C., Nicholas LaBerge, Daniel B. Larremore, Mirta Galesic, Jennie E. Brand, and Aaron Clauset. "Socioeconomic Roots of Academic Faculty." *Nature Human Behaviour* 6 (August 29, 2022): 1625–1633, 10.1038/s41562-022-01425-4.

Nietzel, Michael T. "The Well-Heeled Professoriate: Socioeconomic Backgrounds of University Faculty." *Forbes*, March 28, 2021. www.forbes.com/sites/michaeltnietzel/2021/03/28/the-well-heeled-professoriate-socioeconomic-backgrounds-of-university-faculty/?sh=1efc329c5e22.

Rhodes Trust. "Legacy, Equity, & Inclusion." www.rhodeshouse.ox.ac.uk/impact-legacy/legacy-equity-inclusion/.

Vardaman, Elizabeth. "Recalculating: A Sojourn Down Scholarship Road to the Deep Heart's Core." In *All In: Expanding Access Through Nationally Competitive Awards*, edited by Suzanne McCray. Fayetteville, AK: University of Arkansas Press, 2013.

Chapter 1

What Our Students Don't Know: What Is a Fellowship, and Why Apply for One?

Years before the phrase "first-generation college student" was a widely discussed phenomenon in American universities, one of my advisees remarked that she often felt, in encounters with her classmates, "as if I was hearing a joke and everyone was laughing but me, because I didn't get the punchline."[1] In all the years since, I haven't heard a better description of what it is to feel like a social and intellectual outsider in college.[2] For my advisee, embarrassment, disappointment, and even feelings of betrayal combined in a realization that she felt ill-equipped to absorb the education that was supposed to be there for the taking. Feeling hurt, she was moved to create an informal support group to discuss with her First Gen peers the kinds of issues they faced every day. Within the next several years groups like hers sprouted up across the landscape of higher education, and advisors and administrators became increasingly accustomed to thinking more creatively about how to support them.[3]

My student's experience was an example of what has come to be known as the "hidden curriculum."[4] That is, the "hidden expectations, skill sets, knowledge, and social process[es] ... [as well as] unspoken or implicit values, behaviors, procedures, and norms that exist in the educational setting." If your students don't know what a fellowship is and think of a scholarship narrowly as financial aid to pay their tuition, they're likely unaware of the "hidden curriculum" in its many forms.[5]

As a fellowship advisor, I routinely need to remind myself that no one is born knowing what a fellowship is and that I shouldn't expect my students to see something that is "hidden" unless someone like me points it out to them. But it's also important to keep in mind that the hidden curriculum isn't a conspiracy by people "in the know" to keep useful information from the uninitiated. Rather it is a lack of understanding or even ignorance on the part of teachers, administrators, and peers about what is widely known and what is not, for students who are the first in their family's history to attend college. Still, unintended or not, the hidden curriculum has the effect of making our students feel as though, *because* they aren't privy to the forms of knowledge that constitute it, they don't deserve to be.

THE BASICS

As the fellowships advisor at a university that prides itself on the diversity of its student body, the most common questions I get from students new to the world of scholarships and fellowships are, "What is a fellowship, and why should I apply for one?"; and "What's the difference between a scholarship and a fellowship?"[6] Of course, one of the most striking aspects of a public university is the great scope of student talent and experience it serves. As a teacher or advisor, you encounter the entire spectrum of the student body: from students who are unsure whether college is even right for them to those who seem like they would be intellectually at ease at any one of the nation's most exclusive institutions. So, while it's important to bear this in mind when you talk to a student for the first time so that they don't feel you've underestimated them, I find that to the great majority of students at my university the word "fellowship" sounds alien, even off-putting. I explain to them that while there was at one time a distinction between fellowships and scholarships, this is no longer the case. Today, the words fellowship and scholarship are synonymous, and I use the words interchangeably throughout this book.[7]

The original meaning of the word fellowship in English referred to "a position of dignity, or the emoluments of a 'fellow' in a university, college, or learned society, etc." This definition, which comes from the *Oxford English Dictionary*, sounds fussy and remote. Nevertheless, it combines two of the most significant aspects of its contemporary meaning: the prestige or honor a fellowship bestows on the recipient and the salary (or "stipend") attached to the position.[8] "Fellowship" derived, additionally, from the idea that some collection of people "*in fellowship*" come together for a specified purpose, scholarly or otherwise; but that sense of the word has receded over the years, and it no longer connotes this purpose.[9] The word "scholarship," historically, was often used in combination with "fellowship" but colloquially it is used today to mean support for any kind of academic opportunity. Its meaning is broader than fellowship since it includes not just merit-based financial support but also (and especially) tuition for attendance at a school or college awarded to students who could not otherwise afford to attend. This is the meaning most students associate with the word because it is the term they most commonly encounter as they determine whether, admitted to a college or university, they can afford to attend.

This is another reason I take some time to talk with my students about the meaning of "scholarship" and "fellowship." In fact, this reason arises from a confusion that goes to the heart of why so many students can't imagine why they would go to the trouble of applying for a scholarship: if they are fortunate enough to have most of their tuition and other expenses covered by a scholarship from financial aid at their university, they may not be able to conceive of expending the effort it takes to apply for a nationally competitive scholarship in order to carry out an ambition that doesn't directly move them toward the goal of graduating from college.

For many of my students, whether because of the high cost of college or because of the enormous pressure they feel from family members to be as pragmatic as they can in pursuit of their degrees, any activity that seems like a detour from that goal is deemed a waste of time (or a luxury they can't afford). Their parents or guardians may lack a college degree themselves, have scant money to pay for their children's education, need them to contribute to family income as soon as they graduate from college, or dream that their student will land a well-paying job when they complete their schooling. Many of my students are the children of immigrants who have mortgaged their futures by leaving their home countries to come to the United States. If your students' parents have forsaken their way of life and the proximity of loved ones, then it's likely their sacrifice is top of mind for your students, too, as they move through their college years. Even if that is not the case, it's reasonable for them to feel they need to be laser-focused on getting through college in the least amount of time for the sake of securing a foothold in a profession. However, students who are exclusively oriented to minimizing the amount of time between completing their degrees and getting the first meaningful job after college are likely to be blinded to the many life-changing opportunities made available through fellowships and the value of the recognition they bestow on their recipients.

While nationally competitive scholarships range from tuition assistance to support for independent study, they are all designed to reward the scholarly and intellectual merit of a proposed project, some form of public service, or a student's achievement and academic potential. While the student sitting in front of you may be someone who excels in their courses, they may, nonetheless, underestimate their own potential, achievements, and prospects of winning a fellowship. Many of the students I advise say that the prospect of applying for a fellowship feels so overwhelming that they don't even dare to consider what might be gained if they were to win one. So it's doubly important not to allow them to "self-discourage" or neglect opportunities simply because they are confused about what a fellowship is or don't know anyone who has applied for one.

REASONS FOR APPLYING

After you've explained that the word "scholarship" means more than tuition, your student may only dimly perceive the variety of activities they might subsidize. Study abroad, internships, skill-building conferences, research, travel to archives, participation in academic meetings, partial or full financial support for work toward an advanced degree, participation in a pre-professional or academic support network, preparation for applying to graduate or professional schools—the number and range of opportunities funded by scholarships and fellowships has exploded during the past twenty years and this, of course, can only be news to the great majority of students. And yet, few scholarly experiences your students have in college will have such immediate, tangible benefits as winning a fellowship. The rewards built into the process of applying, moreover—*intrinsic* rewards—begin paying dividends before a student even puts the finishing touches on an application. The primary benefit of applying is that, whether they are successful or not, a student will find that the very act of composing a personal statement and completing an application compels them to begin asking questions of themselves that will set them onto a path of self-discovery. Specifically, this process should lead them, eventually, to understanding and articulating their sense of purpose. This is the most important benefit of the application process, so the second part of this chapter is devoted to the cluster of intrinsic rewards imparted in the doing.

Because a fellowship applicant must aim to create, ideally, a holistic, coherent narrative about themselves that joins their experiences, interests, and skills to their aspirations, they will begin to formulate, both for themselves and for others, a picture of who they are and hope to be—a template, if you will, for their future. I will discuss how to compose this narrative in Chapter 5, where I describe the parts of the personal statement, but for now it's important to understand that a student can use the narrative they develop about themselves not only for their fellowship and graduate school applications but as a compass that will point them toward their present and future goals.[10]

College is a period in a student's life of unprecedented change and inertia. It's difficult for them to find the time (and *most* of us lack the inclination) to sit for any length of time to consider what it all means—one's life—what it adds up to, and to ask themselves, "Where am I going?" Yet the act of completing an application—not just writing the personal statement but providing all the other information required, such as listing one's activities, achievements, jobs, internships, hobbies, and personal obligations—provides a unique occasion for stocktaking, and thus yields a sense of direction and forward motion. Goals are certainly important. When we are young, most of us find we are frequently asked, especially by family and friends, what our goals are. (Unless you are studying something that leads irrefutably to a profession, who has *not* had the experience of reporting to an older family member that you have chosen this or that field of study, only to be asked in return, "What are you going to do with *that?*") Since the beginnings of mass education in the United States, there has been a popular fixation on the relationship of schooling to one's vocational or professional ambitions.[11] As college has come within reach for so many people over the last seventy-five years, so has the notion that its value can and should be measured monetarily.[12] But *fulfillment* arises from working toward the satisfaction of one's purpose in life. Earning a living, of course, is necessary and often important to one's sense of self-worth. However, a sense of purpose, by contrast, is often unfocused, unverbalized, and cognitively confused with *goals*, which, though related, are more readily identified and expressed, acted-upon, achieved (or not), and noted. But what then?

Figure 1.1 Rhodes Scholar Thamara Jean, University of Oxford, 2018. Photograph courtesy of Thamara Jean

In reply to the rhetorical question that I ask my students, "Why should you apply for a fellowship?" my answer is, "Because the act of having to put down in writing not merely what you want to accomplish but why it matters to you, how it relates to who you are, what you have already achieved, and where you are headed is a great start on the lifelong mission of understanding what motivates you and creates meaning for you."

EXTRINSIC REASONS FOR APPLYING FOR FELLOWSHIPS

All the ways a fellowship can promote a student's success I think of as "extrinsic" reasons for applying. I take some time to review with my students the most conspicuous of these reasons because they are more motivating than the less visible, deferred benefits produced by introspection and the kind of intellectual and personal growth entailed by composing essays and addressing the questions posed by fellowship applications. Extrinsic reasons for applying to fellowships consist of the following, which all presume that your student will win an award: (1) to afford an experience they wouldn't otherwise be able to

WHAT IS A FELLOWSHIP, AND WHY APPLY FOR ONE?

participate in; (2) to enhance the likelihood of future success in their discipline broadly and increase the likelihood of future funding for their work; (3) to become a more desirable applicant for graduate or professional school and, ultimately, a job; and (4) to extend and deepen their connections to others in their field—both potential mentors and peers.

1. To afford an experience they wouldn't otherwise be able to participate in: This is the most obvious reason to apply for a fellowship and the chief incentive for most students. Students are often surprised, however, by the range of fellowships available to them. Indeed, the number of opportunities for undergraduates at every level (as I have said earlier) has mushroomed during the past two decades.
2. To enhance the chance of future success: A fellowship marks its recipient as someone whose work has been recognized by authorities in their field as deserving of notice and support. Moreover, a fellowship winner is more likely to meet with success when they apply for future fellowships. Academic scientists typically apply for grant support continuously throughout their careers. First their survival and then their long-term success depends on their ability to bring in outside money to their home institutions. While this "eat what you kill" orientation is more characteristic of the sciences than other fields, scholars in every field distinguish themselves by winning fellowships and can free up time from other obligations by getting financial support from outside of their institutions. While gaining others' high opinion professionally may seem like a distant dream to a student, the recognition conferred by a fellowship at any stage has a kind of "multiplier effect." It brings more and more opportunities the way of its recipient and affords the recipient more latitude to pursue the kind and quality of work they want to do rather than simply what they must do to keep their job. It both enables the recipient to complete work that makes their hiring possible, and in academia, makes it more likely that they'll be promoted and achieve tenure.
3. To become a more desirable candidate: Whether they're applying for an internship, another fellowship, graduate or professional school, or a job, a student should know that a fellowship remains on the recipient's résumé throughout their career and will make them stand out when they seek opportunities of every kind in the future. When they apply for a position, their success in winning fellowships is a testament to others' belief in their future promise and the quality of their work.
4. To extend and deepen connections: Whether they are to be future scholars or professionals, your students will depend throughout most of their careers on the work of others and the relationships they build with older mentors who can show them the way forward. Mentors can reveal the most alluring

aspects of a discipline and its possibilities, as well as its hazards and its most perplexing and intriguing problems. Mentors will testify to the merit of a student's work and speak to their potential. In a different vein but no less important, ultimately, a student's peers, whether they are engaged in some form of collaboration with the student or even if they compete with them in some sense, can help them master and sharpen their command of the fundamentals of their field of study. A student's connections—with both mentors and peers—are often facilitated by fellowships that bring them into contact with people whose ideas enrich or challenge their own.

Finally, I want to highlight one other benefit of winning a scholarship, which applies to many but not all fellowship experiences. Because so many funded opportunities send their recipients abroad, winning a fellowship can help a student create an international network of friends and professional associates that, ideally, will be a lifelong network. I can tell you from many years of advising that there isn't a single student I've worked with who has spent time abroad who failed to appreciate how much the experience helped them understand themselves better, as well as understand what was distinct or even provincial about their own attitudes, culture, and national perspective, what is universal to people everywhere, and how others' opinions, experiences, behaviors, and customs may differ from their own. Spending time abroad makes a student a better citizen of the world, which of course, is increasingly important as we become ever-more reliant on one another globally to adapt, survive, and flourish as human beings. In other words, most students acquire some wisdom and perspective and do a lot of growing up if they're away from their home country even for as a little as a semester. Going abroad may not be a priority for a student at the age of 19 or 20, but it will be a palpable advantage as they begin to evaluate seriously what they want to do with themselves professionally and as they face a series of personal life-course decisions during the decade following college. And most, if not all, international experiences entail improving if not mastering proficiency in another language. Increasingly, every endeavor, whether in law, medicine, business, or academia, seeks out and favors applicants who are multilingual. This just wasn't true in the United States a generation ago, but the ability to function in multiple languages has become a highly desired skill in today's professional job market.

INTRINSIC REASONS FOR APPLYING FOR FELLOWSHIPS

Most fellowship applications will ask an applicant to write about who they are (and implicitly, where they come from), what they care about, why they want the fellowship, and what they will do with it. These questions force a student to take stock of themselves, and the exercise at the end of this chapter will help your students begin to formulate a sense of purpose. We will consider more fully for your students the question "Who are you?" in Chapter 3 because addressing this particular question is at the heart of the personal statement. Between the personal statement and other parts of the application, they'll be asked to list their experiences, accomplishments, awards, recognitions, and qualifications. They also may be asked to consider their goals, in the short, mid, and long term. Some fellowship applications also prompt candidates to envision a "path" to achieving their goals—to imagine both what further education and skills they'll require and what roles they'll need to take on to accomplish their aspirations. They'll be asked to name their skills and what they're good at but also what good they can do; that is, what they have to offer the world. Ultimately, explicitly or not, every fellowship application invites them to contemplate how their actions and beliefs reflect the values of the fellowship they're applying for.

"A RISING MOTION OF SPIRIT"

I've advised students at four different universities, and every year at each campus, it seems, some highly accomplished graduate is invited to return to talk about the secret to their success. Invariably they advise students to follow their "bliss" or discover their "passion." The spirit of this advice hits the mark for many students—a bit of wisdom from someone who once stood in their shoes gives them the ounce of courage they need to dare to be the person they want to become someday. But for others, the advice rings hollow: having achieved success, it seems facile for an accomplished alum to tell people beginning to contemplate possible careers that they should do what most appeals to them without regard for expense or remuneration. It can not only sound like a luxury they can't afford but can seem tone-deaf, too—oblivious to the kinds of sacrifices they and their families have made just to send them to college, quite apart from any career considerations. At the same time, students who belong to the first generation in their family to attend college or whose necessity—whether determined by family finances, citizenship status, or personal obligation—precludes anything but a single-minded vocational approach to college, also deserve the "luxury" of exposure to what a college education makes possible for them. Many aren't even aware of the range and variety of careers they might realize. I wasn't.

As I suggested earlier, at the age of eighteen, I understood somehow (though not concretely) that it would be advantageous to have a college degree, but I had no conception, for instance, until my second year of college what had qualified my professors to teach at the college level. I didn't question it. Their very presence at the front of the classroom was its own legitimation. My high school experience, moreover, had left me fairly indifferent toward college before I even decided to apply. My father's parents were working-class people who limped through the Great Depression. My father and his three brothers each benefitted in various ways from serving in the military and eventually gained a foothold in the expanding middle class of the 1950s and '60s. Still, even by the time I finished high school in the mid-1970s, college had not yet become an indispensable credential—the floor beneath which you could not sink if you sought the financial stability of middle-class existence. In other words, neither my family background nor the state of the US economy (as we perceived it at the time) upheld college as the only viable route to occupational security.

Consequently, I chose the path of least resistance and enrolled in my local community college after high school. My thought was to try it out. Because it was inexpensive and because my parents expected me to pay half of the cost of my college education, if the experiment failed or didn't appeal, I could cut my losses without having invested too much in the attempt. But then the unforeseen happened; during my freshman year, I caught fire academically. Even today it feels somehow self-aggrandizing to say this, but in my second semester I experienced for the first time what A. Bartlett Giamatti once described as "the rising motion of spirit" a liberal education occasions and "the voyage of exploration in freedom that is the development of your own mind."[13] I had always enjoyed learning about the past and had, since grade school, devoured the biographies of notable people throughout history. But in my very first year of college, I had a teacher named John ("Chuck") Chalberg who periodically impersonated characters from American history in his lectures—not just the most recognizable, like Theodore Roosevelt, or clever, like H. L. Mencken, but venomous figures, like the white supremacist villain Edmund Ruffin, who was credited with firing the first shot of the Civil War at Fort Sumter. The humanity and complexity of the past suddenly came alive for me. Under Chalberg's mentoring I applied for and won my first fellowship, a "Youthgrant" sponsored by the National Endowment for the Humanities. This experience further opened a world of intellectual striving to me and the confidence that I could participate, but also, in the rousing rhetoric of Giamatti's urging, the experience of "charting and ordering and dwelling in the land of my own intellect and sensibility, discovering powers I had only dreamed of and mysteries I had not imagined and reaches I had not thought that I could reach."[14] Not only had I discovered my passion but in the process discovered that "bliss" had much to do with mental activity. This was my first glimpse of the possibilities of pursuing scholarship as a way of life.

FROM PASSION TO PURPOSE

"Passion," indeed, is shorthand for much of what fellowship applications are trying to elicit from applicants with their essay prompts, requests for résumés, lists of activities, and descriptions of favorite undergraduate courses.[15] Encouragement to discover one's passion is good advice as far as it goes. It's imperative for students to reflect on what excites and energizes them. Identifying their enthusiasms helps them understand what inspires and motivates them. But more than this, understanding what inspires them enables them to articulate their purpose, and *that* is what should be their ultimate aim. The relationship of passion to commitment in life points to what the applicant cares about; and the things they care about are the wellspring of purpose. In other words, it's important for a student not simply to be aware of what stirs that "rising motion of spirit" within them but to discern connections between their enthusiasms and the commitments they've made, and how they create and sustain meaning in their daily lives.

Remember, however, that the age of the average college student—conventionally between eighteen and twenty-two—is very young to have articulated a purpose in life. Nevertheless, as many of us have experienced, one of the major shifts over the last generation or so is the expectation that our students will know their purpose in the sense of having identified a career and formulated post-college plans as they approach graduation. This pressure "to know" comes primarily from family members and peers rather than teachers, of course, but it's important to be mindful of students' internalized sense of the relationship between their goals and the passage of time. However often our vocational choices fall short of our ideals, "career" for many of our students *implies purpose* in the sense that most professional paths are chosen in hopes of doing some kind of good, providing an important service or being of use to a noble cause, or at the very least, earning an income that will afford a secure, comfortable living, in addition to being a source of lasting fulfillment.

For people of my generation who went to college during the 1970s and the early '80s, there was little expectation that your course of study (apart from pre-medical studies) would cast the future in stone. The ideal college education was a journey of personal, intellectual, social, political, and cultural exploration. College and the several years that followed was a time to try on new versions of oneself—or "selves"—not necessarily dictated by the people who raised you. This ideal has fallen on hard times.[16] Paradoxically, even as the luster of the liberal arts and of college in general has dimmed in popular esteem, the monetary value of the college degree has continued to rise.[17] Broader cultural shifts that celebrate fame, power, and money, as well as the higher cost of college, increasing emphasis on one's educational pedigree, and the willingness to take on huge student loans, have made it difficult for young adults to spend their twenties "following their bliss." Thus, the pressure to pick a profession can make a casualty of purpose. If all your student feels is the weight of family expectation bearing down on them, fear of debt, or the anxiety of choosing the road not taken, their ability to stop and consider *why* they want to follow any particular path may become obscure or so deferred that they don't think seriously about what their purpose is until they are much older; until failure, frustration, or boredom forces them to step back and examine what they are doing with themselves and for others. So, while "passion" can set our students on the path to defining their purpose, it is not the same as "purpose," but rather a source of inspiration that can nudge them in a useful direction until they find their calling.

Pondering the relationship of passion to purpose brings to mind philosopher Agnes Callard's illuminating essay on the nature of a liberal arts education in which she distinguishes between two kinds of self-transformation: self-cultivation and aspiration. For getting from passion to purpose involves an act of transformation. "Self-cultivation," Callard says, occurs when you identify a value and change your behavior to fulfill something you *already* believe in or know to be valuable. As when, for instance, a student decides that, to be an effective leader, they need to be persuasive, and to be persuasive they need to sharpen their rhetorical skills and use of logic, so they join their school's debate team. "Aspiration," on the other hand, is a striving to find something and, *in the finding*, discover what, in retrospect, they come to understand to be the logical consequence of having sought it out. Once blurry, the object of one's aspiration comes into focus, Callard observes. "In the developmental steps that one ends up taking ... territory ... seems to materialize as one advances into it."[18]

For example, I may decide that it's important to me to mentor my students well, so that they feel supported and have the confidence they need to excel and grow. I personally value and understand the importance of good mentoring because it was vital to my own success. So, in part, I hold an image in my mind about what good mentoring consists of based on the example of my own mentors. But the other part of becoming a good mentor may consist of reading books and articles on mentoring to absorb and apply "best practices," or I may even attend workshops on the subject to understand what being a good mentor consists of. However, in the process of mentoring I discover the secret to doing it well: properly assessing and bearing in mind my students' gifts, understanding what they need to work on to improve, listening to learn who they dream of becoming and *why* will optimize their potential. And I discover that the relationship is reciprocal in that I experience the satisfaction of supporting a young person's ability, first, to "walk" and, then, to "run." With each successful step we begin to enjoy a trusting relationship that enables me to offer careful but candid advice, to help the student imagine what's possible for them but to remember always that their decision to go in one direction or another is theirs alone. Ideally, their success surpasses my own, and through their "developmental steps" the object I was seeking—this young person's flourishing—"materializes," as Callard says, and as the "prospect" of what I didn't fully appreciate about the value of mentoring "comes into focus."[19]

An aspirant, says Callard, may orient herself to a new value, one she seeks for its own sake, not because it will serve an aim she valued before. "The purpose of what you are doing can itself be something that you are learning ... and one way that a purpose can guide your behavior is by becoming something you get better and better at grasping." And finally, "what drives [this aspirant] is not the appreciation of those values they already have but the prospect of the (true, complete) appreciation they can see they lack."[20]

While the comparison is imperfect, it's helpful, I think, to briefly revisit the double-sided nature of applying for a fellowship. For the distinction between extrinsic/intrinsic qualities of the experience is analogous to the distinction between self-cultivation and aspiration that Callard details. The extrinsic aspects are instrumental (e.g., securing funding); such aspects all concern an "end" a student values and the means to seek it. The intrinsic aspects of the application process embody a form of aspiration because it is in the process of applying that a student must assess what they care about and why (and what they lack), where they are going (a journey of seeking), and the reason for their quest. The fellowship application process, in this sense, represents a form of self-understanding, which, if you are an applicant, you become, in Callard's phrase, "better and better at grasping."

Callard, of course, describes self-cultivation and aspiration as qualitatively distinct, whereas I suggest the experience of applying for a fellowship engages in both. Why does it matter? What I am arguing here is that the fellowship application inevitably involves, in Callard's words, "developmental steps," which, apart from whether a student wins a fellowship or not, result in moving that student closer to a sense of purpose, which will become their polestar as they seek an intellectual experience and, later, a profession that brings ongoing fulfillment. In other words, *because* the more tangible, goal-seeking aspect of self-cultivation *requires* aspiration, it resolves the tension between effort and expectation: the energy and time expended applying for the fellowship versus the outcome.

PURPOSE

A further word about purpose. I'm not a philosopher or a psychologist—pursuits that typically involve examining the role and cultivation of purpose in our lives—but I know from experience that in order to perform well and to feel fulfilled in my own work, my actions must be connected to an aim and a purpose. An "aim" in our world is to help students apply for fellowships, grow from the experience, and if they are lucky, win, so they can benefit from the opportunity that winning affords. My *purpose* is to help my advisees flourish more generally. Yes, to help them find the success they are seeking, but also to become aware of the ways they need to develop, be reflective and improve so that they can have experiences that amplify their potential: again, in Callard's terms, to "cultivate" themselves. A sense of purpose inhabits what sociologist Max Weber referred to as one's "calling." As developmental psychologist William Damon points out, Weber asserted that all of us possess our own particular callings. I'm not so certain. I have spent the majority of my career in different, if related, positions in higher education, some of which I experienced as "callings"—namely, of my abilities, an appropriate application of what I have to offer, which gave me a real sense of satisfaction and a sense that I was engaged in a form of service to others. "Purpose," which is the foundation of one's calling, according to Damon, "goes beyond personal meaning" and "reaches out to the world beyond the self. It implies a desire to make a difference in the world, perhaps contribute something to others, or create something new."[21] Periodically, in a few of the jobs I have held, I have experienced what I felt was my calling, but even in these jobs, I haven't felt that all the time. "Purpose," continues Damon, "is the final answer to the question, 'Why?' *Why* am I doing this? *Why* does it matter? *Why* is it important for me and for the world beyond me? A purpose is the reason *behind* the immediate goals and motives that drive most of our daily behavior."[22]

Figure 1.2 Thomas Kolokithias, Hunter College, 2019. Photograph by the author

Before we engage the question most central to the personal statement, "Who are you?" which we'll do in Chapter 3, I want to emphasize that it's helpful to think about the intrinsic rewards, values, and reasons we've been contemplating as integral to helping our students understand themselves (who they are). Again, though students don't often reflect on who they are until they are prompted by a fellowship application to put their unformed thoughts into writing, the student's quest to understand how they came to be and where they are going is the most important aspect of the work they will put into applying for a fellowship. By contrast, the extrinsic rewards, values, and reasons associated with applying for a fellowship might easily be mistaken for vanity simply because they bring recognition, esteem, and opportunity. While it's important for your students to be aware of the degree to which they desire to distinguish themselves and succeed professionally, applying for a fellowship is deeply connected to who they want to be, both as a person and as a future professional or scholar. Applying for a fellowship is the proximate cause of their impending self-transformation—the grain of sand embedded in the oyster that stimulates the layers of nacre that will one day form a pearl.

To summarize, it's important for your students to understand that there is value in the simple act of applying for a fellowship—they will grow personally, intellectually, and professionally in ways unique to the demands of the application process. The rewards of winning are mostly unimagined, indeed, unimaginable by them, and exceed the fact of winning itself. This is true for any application that forces the would-be candidate to contemplate who they are, what they are trying to accomplish, why they are applying, and what they will do if they win, whether they are applying for a fellowship or to graduate school.

If your students are the conventional age of most college students (18–22), they may not be accustomed to being asked "what is your purpose in life?" Indeed, the following exercise is a kind of conceit in that many of us don't really understand our purpose until we are much older than twenty or even thirty. However, whether your students are already pointed in the direction of a career or not, it is helpful for them to begin thinking seriously and systematically about what motivates them, why, and as Damon emphasizes, what "good" they are to other people. This exercise will start them on their path to purpose.

> **EXERCISE FOR YOUR STUDENTS: INVENTORY OF PURPOSE**
>
> Ask your students to take the "Youth Purpose Study" questionnaire in the appendix of William Damon's book, *The Path to Purpose*, pp. 183–86. This will help them begin to examine what matters to them and why and how they are pursuing what they care about (or not). It also asks them to consider when certain activities, causes, or issues became important to them, who supports them in engaging in those activities, how they fit into their short-, mid-, and long-range plans, and whether they speak to their sense of purpose as they currently conceive it.

NOTES

1. My former student graduated from Yale College, was a recipient of an NSF–Graduate Research Fellowship, earned a PhD in Sociology at the University of Pennsylvania, and currently works at Meta.
2. For a thoughtful full-length study, see Rachel Gable, *The Hidden Curriculum: First Generation Students at Legacy Universities* (Princeton, NJ: Princeton University Press, 2021), especially chap. 5. Today the phenomenon is so widely recognized that there is an acronym for being the first member in the history of your extended family to attend college—"FGCS." Of course, historically, the first prominent wave of "first-generation college students" came in the wake of World War Two, when the G.I. Bill made college free or affordable for millions of American veterans thereafter. The current experience came about as a result of the reform of immigration laws during the 1960s and the commitment by private universities to "need-blind admissions" and significantly increasing financial aid to students from financially modest backgrounds. FGCSs today come from mostly lower-middle class and working-class families but are often also students of color, immigrants, or rural Americans.
3. Indeed, during my final full year at Brown, the Dean's Office was approached about joining a study being organized by Harvard to survey the first-generation experience, which (with Brown's and Georgetown's participation) produced the First-Generation Student Success Project (2012) and the source material for Gable's fine book. When I arrived at Harvard the next year as Dean of Student Life, one of the first spontaneous student initiatives to emerge was a social support network for first-generation students.
4. Much of what Anthony Jack describes in his intensive analysis of the challenges faced by first-generation, low-income students of color at elite private universities vivifies how students experience the "hidden curriculum," but more important, Jack eloquently unpacks the way that social inequities are experienced often as personal differences in private encounters between Black students at elite institutions. See Anthony Abraham Jack, *The Privileged Poor: How Elite Colleges Are Failing Disadvantaged Students* (Cambridge, MA: Harvard University Press, 2019). And see the preface and the first chapter of Gable's *The Hidden Curriculum*. Gable says, in her preface, on p. ix, that the term "hidden curriculum" was coined by Philip W. Jackson in his *Life in Classrooms* (New York: Holt, Rinehart and Winston, 1968). See also Jessica McCrory Calarco's insightful description of the effects of the hidden curriculum on first-generation students aspiring to graduate school and a career in academia: Jessica McCrory Calarco, *A Field Guide to Grad School: Uncovering the Hidden Curriculum* (Princeton, NJ: Princeton University Press, 2020), 1–9.
5. Merfat Ayesh Alsubaie, "Hidden Curriculum as One of Current Issue of Curriculum," *Journal of Education and Practice* 6, no. 33 (2015): 125, https://files.eric.ed.gov/fulltext/EJ1083566.pdf. Alsubaie refers to an early and influential work on the subject by John P. Miller and Wayne Seller, *Curriculum: Perspectives and Practice* (Toronto: Copp Clark Pitman, 1990). See also McCrory Calarco, *Field Guide to Grad School*, 1.
6. On the diversity of Hunter College as of fall 2021, see "Campus Ethnic Diversity: Regional Universities North," *US News & World Report*, www.usnews.com/best-colleges/rankings/regional-universities-north/campus-ethnic-diversity.

7. Even among those of us who direct fellowships offices, the distinctions between "scholarships," "fellowships," and "grants" is not as clear as one would assume. Early in 2023 the director of a fellowships office wrote to the National Association of Fellowships Advisors (NAFA) listserv asking for a formal definition because they were preparing to address their faculty about the activities of their office, confessing, "I'm new to this role [and wondering therefore], 'Does NAFA have/use specific definitions and distinctions…?'" I thank Michelle Douenias, Senior Program Manager, Luce Scholars Program at The Henry Luce Foundation, for bringing this posting to my attention.
8. *The Compact Edition of the Oxford English Dictionary*, vol. 1 (New York: Oxford University Press, 1971), *s.v.* "fellowship," definition 8.
9. But see McCrory Calarco, *Field Guide to Grad School*, 163, where she makes a distinction between students and professional academics who receive grants or fellowships. The former have no obligation to convene, whereas the latter are often brought together as a group. See also the brief discussion of the terminology in Paul A. Bohlmann and Adonica Y. Lui, *The Harvard College Guide to Grants*, 12th ed. (Cambridge, MA: Harvard University, 2003), v.
10. I don't want to mislead here: the "personal statement" for graduate school is typically brief—about a paragraph of a longer statement of purpose. However, by writing out the kind of personal statement required by a major post-bac fellowship, a student is forced to consider essential questions about motivation and purpose and how these connect to their personal biography. Only then can they effectively distill their ideas down to the one pithy paragraph needed for the graduate school application. See McCrory Calarco, *A Field Guide to Grad School*, 38–39.
11. Maris Vinovskis, "Horace Mann on the Economic Productivity of Education," *New England Quarterly* 43, no. 4 (Dec. 1970): 550–71; David F. Labaree, *How to Succeed in School Without Really Learning: The Credentials Race in American Education* (New Haven, CT: Yale University Press, 1997).
12. In hopes of increasing the accountability of universities and creating a more objective basis for college rankings, President Barack Obama inadvertently accelerated this mentality by promoting a national "scorecard" for colleges that links institutions' rankings to graduates' income, rather than perceived prestige. See Li Zhou, "Obama's New College Scorecard Flips the Focus of Rankings," *The Atlantic*, September 15, 2015, www.theatlantic.com/education/archive/2015/09/obamas-new-college-scorecard-flips-the-focus-of-rankings/405379/. The US Department of Education "College Scorecard" was updated in April 2023 with information on institutional characteristics, enrollment, student aid, costs, student outcomes (earnings one year after graduation), and cumulative debt at graduation; see https://collegescorecard.ed.gov/data/.
13. I first encountered this quote in an essay by Agnes Callard that featured former Yale President A. Bartlett Giamatti's 1983 freshman convocation speech, "The Earthly Uses of a Liberal Education," which is reprinted in A. Bartlett Giamatti, *A Free and Ordered Space: The Real World of the University* (New York: W.W. Norton, 1988), 118–126. See Agnes Callard, "Liberal Education and the Possibility of Valuational Progress," *Social Philosophy & Policy* 34, no. 2 (Winter 2017): 17.
14. Giamatti, "Earthly Uses of a Liberal Education," 119.

15. But see my advice in Chapter 5, "Framing the Narrative," about students' avoiding the use of the word "passion" in their personal statements.
16. If you are interested in learning more about this trend, see Johann N. Neem's book, *What's the Point of College? Seeking Purpose in an Age of Reform* (Baltimore, MD: Johns Hopkins University Press, 2019).
17. Collin Binkley and Hannah Fingerhut, "AP-NORC Poll: Many Youths Say High School Diploma Is Enough," Associated Press, November 11, 2019, https://apnews.com/article/education-us-news-ap-top-news-politics-economy-d95f28b579a64c888c74b016ebedd002.

    In fact, however, a 2016 study showed that average annual income of a college graduate is 46% higher than the average annual income of a worker with only a high school diploma. See Association of Public & Land-Grant Universities, "How Does a College Degree Improve Graduates' Employment and Earnings Potential?" www.aplu.org/projects-and-initiatives/college-costs-tuition-and-financial-aid/publicuvalues/employment-earnings.html, and Kim Parker, "The Growing Partisan Divide in Views of Higher Education," Pew Research Center, August 19, 2019, www.pewresearch.org/social-trends/2019/08/19/the-growing-partisan-divide-in-views-of-higher-education-2/. Also see Anthony P. Carnevale, Ban Cheah, Martin Van Der Werf, *ROI of Liberal Arts Colleges: Value Adds Up Over Time* (Washington, DC: Georgetown University Center on Education and the Workforce, 2020), https://cew.georgetown.edu/wp-content/uploads/Liberal-Arts-ROI.pdf, which shows that there are differential earnings outcomes over ten years, depending on the institution attended.
18. My emphasis; see Callard, "Liberal Education," 18.
19. Callard, "Liberal Education," 21.
20. Callard, "Liberal Education," 20–21.
21. Here I am paraphrasing William Damon's summary of Max Weber's description of "calling." See Damon, *Path to Purpose*, 33.
22. Damon, *Path to Purpose*, 33–34.

WORKS CITED

Alsubaie, Merfat Ayesh. "Hidden Curriculum as One of Current Issue of Curriculum." *Journal of Education and Practice* 6, no. 33 (2015): 125–28. https://files.eric.ed.gov/fulltext/EJ1083566.pdf.

Association of Public & Land-Grant Universities. "How Does a College Degree Improve Graduates' Employment and Earnings Potential?" www.aplu.org/our-work/4-policy-and-advocacy/publicuvalues/employment-earnings/.

Binkley, Collin, and Hannah Fingerhut. "AP-NORC Poll: Many Youths Say High School Diploma Is Enough." *Associated Press*, November 11, 2019. https://apnews.com/article/education-us-news-ap-top-news-politics-economy-d95f28b579a64c888c74b016ebedd002.

Bohlmann, Paul A., and Adonica Y. Lui. *The Harvard College Guide to Grants*. 12th ed. Cambridge, MA: Harvard University, 2003.

Callard, Agnes. "Liberal Education and the Possibility of Valuational Progress." *Social Philosophy & Policy*, 34, no. 2 (Winter 2017). 10.1017/S0265052517000188.

"Campus Ethnic Diversity: Regional Universities North." *US News & World Report*. www.usnews.com/best-colleges/rankings/regional-universities-north/campus-ethnic-diversity.

Carnevale, Anthony P., Ban Cheah, Martin Van Der Werf. *ROI of Liberal Arts Colleges: Value Adds Up Over Time*. Washington, DC: Georgetown University Center on Education and the Workforce, 2020. https://cew.georgetown.edu/wp-content/uploads/Liberal-Arts-ROI.pdf.

The Compact Edition of the Oxford English Dictionary. New York: Oxford University Press, 1971.

Damon, William. *The Path to Purpose: How Young People Find their Calling in Life*. New York: Free Press, 2009.

Gable, Rachel. *The Hidden Curriculum: First Generation Students at Legacy Universities*. Princeton, NJ: Princeton University Press, 2021.

Giamatti, A. Bartlett. "The Earthly Uses of a Liberal Education." In *A Free and Ordered Space: The Real World of the University*. New York: W.W. Norton, 1988.

Jack, Anthony Abraham. *The Privileged Poor: How Elite Colleges Are Failing Disadvantaged Students*. Cambridge, MA: Harvard University Press, 2019.

Jackson, Philip W. *Life in Classrooms*. New York: Holt, Rinehart and Winston, 1968.

Labaree, David F. *How to Succeed in School Without Really Learning: The Credentials Race in American Education*. New Haven, CT: Yale University Press, 1997.

McCrory Calarco, Jessica. *A Field Guide to Grad School: Uncovering the Hidden Curriculum*. Princeton, NJ: Princeton University Press, 2020.

Miller, John P., and Wayne Seller. *Curriculum: Perspectives and Practice*. Toronto: Copp Clark Pitman, 1990.

Neem, Johann N. *What's the Point of College? Seeking Purpose in an Age of Reform*. Baltimore, MD: Johns Hopkins University Press, 2019.

Parker, Kim. "The Growing Partisan Divide in Views of Higher Education." Pew Research Center, August 19, 2019. www.pewresearch.org/social-trends/2019/08/19/the-growing-partisan-divide-in-views-of-higher-education-2/.

US Department of Education. "College Scorecard." https://collegescorecard.ed.gov/data/.

Vinovskis, Maris. "Horace Mann on the Economic Productivity of Education." *New England Quarterly* 43, no. 4 (Dec. 1970): 550–71.

Zhou, Li. "Obama's New College Scorecard Flips the Focus of Rankings." *The Atlantic*, September 15, 2015. www.theatlantic.com/education/archive/2015/09/obamas-new-college-scorecard-flips-the-focus-of-rankings/405379/.

Chapter 2

Common Denominators: What It Takes to Be a Successful Applicant

What do scholarship winners have in common? To illustrate, I offer a case study of a student who, despite long odds, prevailed in her quest for a nationally competitive scholarship. Aspects of her life are patently unusual but others—her personal qualities, forms of support she received, out-of-classroom experiences, and the decisions she made from semester to semester—are common to most successful applicants and, thus, instructive. Emily Johnson, a rising senior (at the time of this writing) and a first-generation college, low-income student, was brought to my attention by a good friend, a history professor at Ohio State who works with Fulbright applicants through the university's fellowships office.[1] Emily won the Beinecke Scholarship in her junior year, an award that subsidizes students with high financial need during the first two years of graduate training. In most large universities, a student like Emily could easily fall through the cracks. Were you to meet her, apart from her refreshing affability and light-hearted demeanor, she might not strike you as exceptional. In other words, she'd be easy to overlook at an institution with hundreds of potential applicants. And yet her story, so unlikely for someone poised to enter a PhD program in sociology after graduation, reveals essential patterns underlying student success.

Born in Huntington, West Virginia, a small city in the shadow of the Appalachian Mountains, Emily grew up on the other side of the border Huntington shares with Chesapeake, Ohio, a village of 700 people. Her mother raised Emily by herself and they migrated across the Ohio River just after Emily finished kindergarten. Moving became a refrain in Emily's young life: even as they remained in the Chesapeake area, they moved two-dozen times before Emily finished high school; and after she finished seventh grade, they were homeless for a time and had to stay with her grandmother. Despite the precarity of their existence, Emily's mother always told her how smart she is and how important it was that she attend college one day. Yet when it came time to apply to college, the prospect seemed daunting given that every college had an application fee.

Living in Ohio, she dreamed of attending Ohio State but almost didn't apply because she couldn't afford the fee and didn't think she'd get in. At this point, her best friend's mother, who had supported Emily and her mother materially and emotionally in times of need, told Emily she *had* to apply.

In her first year at Ohio State, Emily's goal was academic survival. She was determined, she said, "just to pass her classes" and do whatever she could to prove to herself that she could. This was during the pandemic, and though she was living on campus, most of her classes were held remotely. Stymied by calculus, she failed her first exam. But she worked with the university's math tutors through the rest of that semester, aced the final exam, and got a B for the course. This proved to Emily that she could succeed in college if she just tried hard enough and used the academic resources available to her.

I asked Emily why she sought help, pointing out that commonly, students whose parents hadn't attended college are reluctant to get help, thinking it a sign of weakness, proof that they can't do the work and that they don't belong.[2] Emily said that in addition to the confidence her mother instilled in her, "I've also had *a lot* of teachers in my life who advocated for me through elementary, middle, and high school. I think that helped me to feel supported by teachers, in general, and comfortable reaching out to them." But she also reflected that in the back of her mind, "I just knew I had to succeed because this was the only chance I had at *not* living life the way I [had] in my childhood."[3]

Early on at Ohio State she took an eye-opening sociology course on social stratification that helped her understand her family's financial straits in broader, historical terms, and became interested in studying poverty. Her sociology teacher became a mentor and urged her to take a social science research methods course during her sophomore year. This course gave Emily the tools she needed to understand the social and economic operations of social stratification in the United States and the confidence to excel in upper-level sociology courses. Her mentor told the department's Director of Undergraduate Studies about Emily's interest in sociological research. He soon offered to supervise her work, since her interest in education and inequality overlapped with his own research on poverty. He began mentoring her too and helped her map out her research.

A few other seemingly unrelated experiences during Emily's sophomore year set her on her current path. On the heels of her success in calculus and armed with insight into the underlying sociological causes of poverty, she founded an honor society for first-generation college students at Ohio State. Strength in numbers. Making legible the hidden curriculum. She also studied abroad in her sophomore year, becoming not just the first in her family to attend college but the first to have a passport. She visited thirteen countries that semester. This gave Emily a glimpse of the bigger life that awaited her, if she worked toward it. And finally, that same year Emily joined an organization called the "Buckeye Leadership Fellows." The experience reinforced her growing self-confidence by teaching its members leadership skills, ways to understand their own capacities, and how to bring out the abilities of those around them. Going into junior year, Emily knew that she wanted to go to graduate school to explore the social and economic forces that have trapped people like her in Appalachia in poverty for generations. When the Beinecke Scholarship appeared on the Leadership Fellows' listserv, it caught Emily's eye because it seemed to describe her. By that point she had spoken with her mentors about her growing desire to go to graduate school in sociology, and the Beinecke, she realized, would make that path much easier. So she applied, was nominated by her university, and won.

Because students can only be nominated for the Beinecke during their junior year of college, they have to know at least by the beginning of junior year that their ambition is to earn a PhD or other terminal degree in an academic discipline other than science. But just as important is the ability to field three strong letters of recommendation from faculty who can speak to a candidate's potential as a future scholar in their chosen field. This is difficult at any university but especially at such a large school like Ohio State and especially when your first year consists mostly of online learning. Emily needed to find faculty to support her ambition. She had two solid recommenders and they helped her recruit another. Gaining the faith of her mentors made it possible to persuade a third professor to sign on to her research and ultimately to furnish the third letter she needed for the Beinecke.[4]

I asked Emily how she had approached this challenge. She reflected that despite her relative disadvantage while growing up she had learned to identify and trust the important adults in her life, starting with her mother, her teachers, and her best friend's mother, her sociology teacher, then her departmental advisor, and her undergraduate thesis advisor. These relationships gave her reason to believe in her own emerging skills and intellectual interests. But along the way she also learned, she says, "the importance of knowing yourself and understanding your identity." Having a clear sense of who she was helped Emily realize what drives her intellectual curiosity generally and, specifically, what fuels her keen interest in poverty research and social stratification. Obviously, the excellence of her work impressed her teachers, but in the end, she found that they were willing to go the extra mile for her because of her evident ambition and determination.

There are several aspects of Emily's story that are arresting in their uniqueness, and it possesses, of course, inherent appeal as an academic "rags to riches" narrative. These aspects are readily apparent to anyone hearing the details of her path from kindergarten to college. But Emily's story also represents the experiences and behaviors common to all students who succeed in college. Emily's example is illuminating: understanding where she comes from and who she is; being supported by a series of adults in her life and learning to transfer their support and her trust in them to other adults over the course of her college career; being able to step back from her own situation to understand it as a product of larger forces that she could address herself, first by studying it formally, and second, by gathering students on her campus whose backgrounds drew them together to support one another. In effect, she created her own leadership experience. It was organic, springing from a desire to satisfy a common need that was personal and also widely shared. Emily was rewarded for her intellectual curiosity and harnessed it to feed her scholarly imagination and appetite for hard work.

*

As we know, but I think rarely make explicit, students who win scholarships tend to have several things in common, many of which Emily's qualities and actions exemplify. Not all of the attributes listed below characterize every successful applicant, and some scholarships strongly emphasize some subset of these qualities over others. But the following list represents the majority of distinctions and experiences that scholarship committees seek in their most outstanding candidates. Before discussing each of these in turn, I want to stress the importance of one of the last items on this list—"experience applying for fellowships"—for it should suggest two things: (1) Applicants who eventually succeed *learn* from the experience of applying for fellowships, that is, they learn both from their mistakes and from their successes. (2) Successful candidates have all failed before they succeeded, and many of us have failed many times. Anyone who applies for a fellowship has to embrace the fact that because these opportunities attract legions of applicants, all of whom hope that their efforts will repay them, the great majority of applications will be rejected, and theirs may be among them. Understanding that rejection is normal is necessary, because if your students don't take this knowledge to heart, they will likely become discouraged and talk themselves out of ever applying for another fellowship again. Help them understand that rather than feeling discouraged by failure they should use it to motivate themselves to try again and do better.

I also remind my students that, win or lose, there is a significant measure of luck involved in the selection process. Scholarship committees work thoughtfully and diligently to identify the best applicants. As we've all seen, even if your students find themselves among the handful of finalists for a fellowship, any number of factors can tip the balance in their favor, or conversely, weigh against them in the end. It's best to know that at a certain point, luck comes into play, so they should just be grateful if it works out. Further, they need to understand that if it doesn't, they should explore how they might improve their approach to the next application and quickly get past their disappointment, so that the next time they apply, preparation, discernment, and good fortune may converge in their favor.

A final word following from this point: it's best to begin early; that is, your students should start applying for scholarships as soon as they get to college.

Most universities have abundant scholarships that they award to their students internally (i.e., within the college) and they tend to increase in number as students work their way toward senior year. Some merit scholarships are awarded at the college or university level (e.g., by the dean's office or financial aid), some by field (humanities, social sciences, art, or math and science), others are awarded within academic departments (History, Philosophy, Biology, etc.). Still others are for special purposes, such as studying abroad, independent study, public service, and so on.

Your office is usually the best place to learn about these awards. But because the culture of institutions varies widely across higher education, information about awards is often radically decentralized, difficult to collect and maintain. If you don't have the resources to keep current with your institution's internal scholarships, your students can do it themselves. Once they've declared a major make sure they talk to their major's advisor or to the department's administrator about the nature of funding available through their department. The most numerous scholarships of any kind nationally are for studying abroad, whether for language learning, cultural exchange, or internships. I'll discuss study abroad further (below) as a great place to begin your students' scholarship searches.

Let's now turn to the factors, qualities, and experiences that most major fellowship winners have in common:

1. Intellectual curiosity and academic excellence
2. Mentoring
3. Leadership experience
4. Extensive extracurricular experience and sustained engagement in a few activities
5. Outstanding letters of recommendation
6. An articulated purpose
7. Skillful writing
8. Study abroad and proficiency in a second language
9. Experience applying for scholarships
10. Ability to make a coherent and compelling case ("connect the dots")[5]

1. INTELLECTUAL CURIOSITY AND ACADEMIC EXCELLENCE

The first and most important quality that any academic fellowship seeks in its candidates is intellectual curiosity. An outstanding grade point average and academic accolades, such as *Phi Beta Kappa*, your college's dean's list, membership in honors programs, either in the student's major, or college-wide, and prizes for the best essay or senior thesis, etc., are each indicators of academic excellence, but they are not synonymous with intellectual curiosity. Generally, fellowship committees expect their best candidates to have a grade point average above 3.5, and some (e.g., Marshall and Rhodes) have a minimum cut-off of 3.7. However, for many language scholarships somewhere around 3.0 is sufficient.

An intellectually curious student is someone who reads widely and reads beyond what's assigned in their coursework—someone who thinks synthetically, linking ideas across fields. A student who seeks out their professors to talk about their research beyond the four corners of the particular subject they're teaching displays intellectual curiosity. So does a student who is well-informed about what's going on in the world of politics, culture, and the arts. Intellectual curiosity can be conveyed through a student's course selection or by independent study (e.g., the capstone for the major), the personal statement and statement of purpose in the fellowship application, or by the letters of recommendation submitted on a student's behalf.

What Your Students Can Do Now

Stay current with the news, not just in the United States but in the world. Take the *New York Times* Weekly Quiz routinely (for instance) to test their knowledge of current events. Read both fiction and nonfiction. For ideas about what to read, it can be helpful to listen to the *New York Times Book Review* podcast and other publications' "best of" listings. Make a habit of going to museums with friends and talk about what they see, what interests them, and why it moves them if it does: activities like this promote intellectual and cultural curiosity. Every university has a speakers series that hosts notable artists, politicians, and intellectuals. Your students should treat this kind of forum like another course in their schedule and attend on a regular basis. If there is a reception afterward, you should encourage them to visit and talk to other guests.

2. MENTORING

Identifying mentors is fundamental to your students' evolving understanding of who they are; mentors promote direction and momentum in their intellectual development. Richard Light says that his advice to students to go find mentors is "the single most important piece of advice I can possibly give to new advisees."[6] It's imperative that students begin to know their teachers early in their time at college. Instructors will connect your students with other colleagues in their field and help them explore the most interesting and dynamic dimensions of their disciplines.[7] Cultivating mentors early will also ensure that your students have faculty who know them longitudinally and can talk later about their evolution as thinkers and even as a future contributors to their fields of study. Mentors will also be able to support your students' applications for fellowships with letters of recommendation as they progress toward graduation.

When I was in college, I didn't understand the purpose of getting to know my teachers or why they would have any interest in knowing me. Whether it was because neither of my parents had taken a traditional path through college or because I went to college in the Midwest, somehow it felt inappropriate to me to cultivate relationships with teachers outside their lectures, even though they were obliged to keep office hours for the very purpose of making time for students to consult with them. My conception of what was supposed to transpire in office hours, however, was confined to asking about something I didn't understand in a lecture or going over my wrong answers on an exam or talking about a paper I was planning to write.

In *The Hidden Curriculum*, Gable cites several examples of First Gen students she interviews as similarly mystified about the role of office hours and how to make best use of them. But more fundamentally, the students she quotes describe, in ways that are all too familiar, feeling that they weren't deserving of their professors' time, finding conversations with their professors halting and awkward or that getting to know their professors outside the lecture hall or classroom was somehow "cheating" the other students in the class. In the Midwest (and many other parts of the US), there is, moreover, a strong egalitarian ethos of maintaining fairness in the distribution of assets, whatever form they take. Getting more of my professors' time than other students felt somehow like gaining an unfair advantage over them in the context of this deeply embedded cultural ethos. The First Gen students in Gable's book, though attending highly selective universities on the Eastern Seaboard, expressed similar sentiments, not only about cultivating mentors but about help-seeking, group study, and other means of promoting academic success as well.[8] Yet once they learned the importance of mentors, it was the key that unlocked their transformation as learners and gave them "permission" to see themselves as future scholars-in-the-making.

What Your Students Can Do Now

Suggest that they sit toward the front of the classroom if they're in a large lecture hall. Arrive for class early. Ask questions and respond to questions if the lecturer invites them to. Try their best to take small, seminar-style classes. If your college offers first-year seminars, your students should be sure to take one. Language courses tend to be small and meet frequently, so they are a great way for students to get to know a teacher early in their time at college.[9] They should go to instructors' office hours to get to know their professors and ensure that their professors get to know them. Follow Richard Light's advice to find and cultivate one mentor each semester; i.e., choose one professor whose office hours they will attend regularly. Read something their professors have published recently, take notes on it, and be prepared to discuss it in their meeting. Help your students understand that their relationship with any potential mentor is a two-way street. It is up to the student to take the initiative and their responsibility to maintain the relationship over time.[10]

3. LEADERSHIP EXPERIENCE

Most major fellowships seek candidates who have demonstrated leadership in some significant fashion. The application for the Marshall Scholarship, which like the Truman requires a letter of recommendation that specifically addresses the candidate's leadership experience and potential, cites the most familiar markers of leadership in its application: having the "ability to deliver results"; "organizing, mobilizing or inspiring others"; being someone "likely to attain a position of influence in his/her field of expertise"; having "demonstrated courage of conviction, persistence, and determination in the pursuit of ... goals," "creativity and innovation in the candidate's approach to answering questions or solving problems," "evidence of a strong desire to contribute to society," and "impact on other people."[11] Conventional leadership roles consist of holding an office in a student organization (president, vice-president, etc.); leadership of student government; serving as executive editor of a school newspaper, yearbook, political or literary magazine; club leadership; or captaining a sports team. All are widely recognized leadership roles. Even more impressive, of course, is "founder" or "founding member" of an organization, which not only demonstrates initiative but also awareness of the need to address a particular problem. Experiences like these present concrete examples for a recommender to offer as evidence of the applicant's promise as a future leader.

More and more fellowships, however, recognize holistic forms of leadership, characterized by soft skills, collaboration, engaged humility, and reflective practice without benefit of a formal title. The Luce Scholarship, for instance, exemplifies this multidimensional approach, describing leadership as requiring: "flexibility and the ability to adapt to unforeseen circumstances ... [and] the discernment to recognize situations where leading may involve being less forceful and instead observing and learning." The scholarship seeks "leaders who can navigate complex challenges with adaptability, open-mindedness, and a willingness to continuously learn and grow."[12]

The Schwarzman Scholarship, which like the Truman and Marshall stresses leadership ability and experience in their selection criteria, offers a highly detailed description of this type of leadership in one of the major essay questions in their application. The essay asks applicants to contemplate various forms of leadership in describing themselves: ways in which the candidate has used their "intellectual/analytical abilities to identify and understand challenges and opportunities, envision solutions, take initiative to act, inspire others to join an effort, and push through resistance and/or challenges to reach results." It goes on to ask the applicant to discuss how they might have initiated change, inspired teamwork, or "helped a group face a challenge and overcome it." Can they show how their involvement in a group activity enabled the group to reach a goal or changed other people's minds?[13]

Figure 2.1 Gerson Borrero, Hunter College, 2019. Photograph by the author

We often think of "natural leaders" as people who routinely step in to give direction to whatever group they're a part of. Their effectiveness, however, can be mixed if their motives arise more from a need to receive recognition or to be in charge than from a desire for the group to succeed in its task or mission. But again, another, usually more successful kind of leader is someone who emerges to lead in response to a particular circumstance, taking the lead where it's clear that initiative is called for, or is urged to step forward by their peers. It should be noted here, too, that some scholarships greatly value the kind of leadership exhibited in the classroom by outstanding students, or the kind of "thought leadership" they may express through their written work as scholars with the potential to be innovators in their academic discipline.

Finally, while being head of the student government at a college or university is impressive, fellowship committees will often press a candidate during an interview to learn whether and what exactly they accomplished while they held the title of "president." Your students, therefore, should understand that a title may attract special scrutiny, and they need to be prepared to describe in detail exactly what they accomplished in that role.

What Your Students Can Do Now

We've already reviewed all the different kinds of activities that a student can engage in beginning in the first year of college. Each of these activities requires someone to lead it, so each represents a future leadership opportunity. Moreover, it's important for your students to understand that leadership is not an inborn ability but is learned, like so many of the other qualities articulated here, and it can be practiced—whether in class by raising their hand and engaging actively in discussion, by adding their voices and energy to group projects, and in the way they conduct themselves in everyday life. Your students, however, should also think carefully about their motives for joining any group. If it's one they truly care about, they can start practicing leadership from the very start simply by "showing up." Participating, volunteering, and *doing the work* of the organization not only sets a good example, it invests the student in the goals and purpose of the group. Their work may be rewarded with a leadership position at some point. But if not, they should remember all the ways one can lead simply by influencing the way others think or by contributing a unique point of view, overcoming a challenge, or inspiring others to join in—all of the kinds of "soft" skills articulated above by the Luce and Schwarzman Scholarships.

4. EXTENSIVE EXTRACURRICULAR EXPERIENCE AND SUSTAINED ENGAGEMENT IN A FEW ACTIVITIES

A number of fellowships particularly prize candidates who demonstrate "energy" and "personal ambition." Sustained involvement in social and political issues as well as interests that synthesize classroom learning with the world beyond the four walls of the university often evince both of these qualities. As we touched on above, most opportunities for leadership available to college students exist in extra- and co-curricular activities but these are, preeminently, arenas of "energy" and "ambition." They also signal intellectual and cultural curiosity. The following activities are typically available at most college campuses or nearby: community service, public service, club membership, affinity group organizations, participation in nationally recognized civic education programs (e.g., debate, Model UN, Model Congress, Mock Trial, etc.), research assistantships, teaching assistantships, peer advising, residential counseling, student government, college/university committee work, writing or editing for student publications, art, music, theatre, dance, and peer education, and employment.

Moreover, if you are in a major city and your school allows your students to get credit for internships, encourage them to begin applying for internships in their first couple of semesters. If opportunities for internships are not widely available in your college's town and your students typically can only perform internships during the summer months, urge your first-year students to think about applying for internships in their home towns where they will be more likely to find one. Many of the most desirable internships during the summers are in major cities, and most students won't be considered for them until the summer between their junior and senior years. Extracurricular experiences give your students helpful professional experience, enable them to cultivate potential mentors, and build their résumés. They also provide insight into ways they can combine what they're learning in the classroom with the kind of careers they might want to pursue after college. If they are in the sciences, to be competitive for fellowships they need to have experience in a lab and have spent significant time learning techniques and participating in a lab's experiments.

What Your Students Can Do Now

If they were in Model UN, Model Congress, Mock Trial, or debate in high school, your students may have already been approached by a student or organization at your college about joining their activity even before they matriculated. While some organizations are more difficult to join than others, the lifeblood of college clubs and organizations is the entering cohort of students, and recruiting can be intense. Once students are comfortable with their workload at college and feel ready to branch out, they should join whatever organizations have most appeal. Typically, leadership of any college organization comes from the junior class. This is because, as seniors, students are all focused on what they'll be doing after college and don't have time to give to their organizations in the same way. This means that the earlier your students start putting in time with an organization, the more likely they'll be tapped to lead it as they rise from sophomore to junior year.

As with the process of applying for fellowships, each extracurricular organization imparts both extrinsic and intrinsic rewards. By participating and doing an organization's work, a student will build a portfolio of activities that demonstrates energy, engagement, and outward focus. In some cases, their involvement will put them on a path to leadership. But participation also builds their social and cultural network, exposes them to new ideas and ways of thinking, gives them experience working productively in a group, and awareness of other opportunities.

5. OUTSTANDING LETTERS OF RECOMMENDATION

While letters of recommendation in support of fellowship applications are written with the understanding that they are confidential, this doesn't mean your student can't contribute to the effectiveness of letters written on their behalf. Obviously, they can't alter whatever opinion their referees have formed of them, but they can choose their recommenders with care and they can discuss with them which aspects of their candidacy they hope their recommenders will address. The best letters of recommendation are ones that describe the student's qualities and accomplishments in detail, contextualize their achievements by comparing them with their peers, and speak knowledgeably about the arc of their development and future trajectory. It is optimal for students to ask for letters from teachers in whose courses they have earned an "A," teachers they have taken more than one course with and have spoken to on numerous occasions outside of class (in office hours, labs, etc.), and teachers (or supervisors) who have known them over a period of time. Unlike applications for graduate study, where they need letters exclusively from ladder faculty who offer the best mixture of familiarity with the student and reputation in their field of study, for most fellowships it's sufficient that the teacher's field of scholarship is relevant to the area the student wants to pursue during their fellowship and that they know the student well. Some fellowships specify the number and type of letters an applicant must submit (academic and otherwise); others will ask them to identify referees to speak to specific qualities valued by the scholarship: e.g., leadership, public service, academic promise. The point is that the student's selection of referees to ask for a fellowship application is different from whom they might ask for graduate study, and they need to understand whether the scholarship requires specific kinds of recommenders.

What Your Students Can Do Now

Again, they should cultivate relationships with potential mentors/recommenders over a period of time. This means maintaining relationships by returning to their teachers or supervisors to talk to them about their progress, any significant changes in their course of study, and their aspirations. Even if they are no longer taking courses with a professor they consider a mentor, they should be sure to stay in touch with them. A student doesn't want to be in the position of asking someone for a recommendation after more than a semester has passed since they last spoke. Once they've decided to request a letter, they should make an appointment with their potential recommender so that they can ask for the recommendation in person. Because this is usually not possible in the summer, a student needs to plan far enough ahead so that they can arrange a meeting before the summer begins. In their meeting they want to talk about the purpose of the fellowship, why they're applying for it, and why they think they would be a worthy candidate. Also they should be certain to discuss their recommender's role as a letter-writer. If the letter-writer advised the student's senior thesis, then the letter should obviously be about the student's strengths as a researcher, thinker, and writer. If the student asks a referee to write about their leadership qualities, they should be sure to bring a copy of their personal statement and résumé and discuss the fact that the fellowship stresses leadership; they should point out areas where they exercised leadership that their recommender might not be aware of, apart from the leadership role in which they've observed the student.

If the recommender already has a letter for the student on file and it's not possible to meet in person, then it's acceptable to craft a polite email to request another reference, being sure to truly *ask* for a letter without conveying a sense of expectation that they will provide it. It's important that a student's potential recommenders feel comfortable saying that they don't know the student well enough to write a recommendation and that the student understands that. The student should say something like: "I'm wondering whether you feel you could provide me with a strong letter of reference for X fellowship?" Make sure recommenders are aware of the due date and how to submit their letter. After the recommender agrees to write on the student's behalf, your student should send that person the following information:

- Brief description of the fellowship and a link where they can find more information
- Reminder about anything you or your student think the recommender should stress
- Draft of the student's personal statement, if at all possible, or at least an informal letter about the scholarship they are seeking and why
- Best paper the student wrote for the letter-writer, ideally a copy with the instructor's comments
- List of courses they took with the professor and other courses in that professor's department
- Their transcript
- Their résumé, for further background
- Best contact information

6. AN ARTICULATED PURPOSE

For "purpose-driven" scholarships, like the Truman, Humanity-in-Action, the Samvid, and the Udall scholarships (to name just a few) the candidate's "purpose" is preordained by their interest in the scholarship itself: the scholarships mentioned above are, respectively, for public service, human rights, "driving positive impact for society," and concern for the environment. However, for most fellowships, the candidate's "purpose" is the most elusive of qualities sought by selection committees but also among the most important.

We will address this attribute in more detail later in this book; however, apart from "purpose-driven" fellowships, all others will expect the applicant to elucidate their purpose in the personal statement and other essays. For these fellowships, most of that work will be done in describing the "intellectual mission" of the project they are undertaking and how it connects with who they are, what motivates them, and how they envision their future.[14]

What Your Students Can Do Now

Your students should spend some time methodically working through Damon's "Inventory of Purpose" exercise referenced at the end of Chapter 1. The point of the exercise is to help your students identify what they really care about, what motivates them, what their goals are, and what brings them the most satisfaction.

7. SKILLFUL WRITING

Your student's personal statement should feature their very best writing. As I will argue in Chapter 5, while everything else they submit as part of their application is unalterable at the point of application, their personal statement is the last component they have the power to make better and their best chance to convince their readers that they deserve their support. If a student is a more skillful writer than other candidates, this is their opportunity to tip the balance in their favor. But your student cannot become a good writer on the day they begin writing their fellowship applications. They need to begin developing their writing skills during their very first semester of college, if possible. It's human nature for us to avoid what we're not good at, but no matter what discipline and no matter what future profession a student pursues, if they can write well, they will get better jobs, get promoted, and continue to be given more and better opportunities. This is as true in science as it is in other fields. College is your students' best and last chance to improve their writing through sustained critique, so they should be urged not to squander it.

What Your Students Can Do Now

Take courses that require them to write and provide them with detailed criticism of their writing. In addition to courses that explicitly teach writing, humanities courses are most likely to provide instructor commentary on how to improve one's writing because humanities disciplines (Literature, Philosophy, History, Classics, Drama, Art History, Music, Journalism) generally expect their faculty to assign significant writing, give detailed attention to student writing, and assign extended reading. Encourage students interested in politics, literature, and the arts to join your college's newspaper or its politics, arts, literary, opinion, and public policy magazines.

8. STUDY ABROAD AND PROFICIENCY IN A SECOND LANGUAGE

Nothing expands students' awareness of their own cultural blind spots, appreciation of divergent viewpoints, or empathy with others and understanding of themselves as a study abroad program. There are more opportunities to win a scholarship to study abroad than any other kind of scholarship. And while it's possible for your student to study abroad without knowing the language of their destination, their experience will be less rich, less meaningful, less enduring than if they have had at least some course work in the language. Fellowship committees look for candidates who can connect ideas across disciplines, geographical borders, and cultures. They want synthetic, creative thinkers who have perspective on themselves and their place in the world. In every profession in the most dynamic sectors of the economy, proficiency in a second language is becoming a requirement. While many universities mandate proficiency at the intermediate level for graduation (or for permission just to study abroad), the fact is, to be competitive in a job market that is only becoming more international, it's foolish of your students not to take advantage of the fact that college is likely their last opportunity to acquire or perfect their mastery of a second language.

For students who have spent little or no time abroad, an added dividend is that studying abroad will force them to become more self-reliant and resourceful in their approach to practical problems as they figure out how to navigate foreign cities, shop for and make daily meals, routinely encounter strangers whose expressions they won't fully comprehend, and with whom they must work to make themselves understood. A consequence of this spell of independence will be an increase in their self-confidence when they return to their home campus, a heightened focus, an enhanced sense of belonging, and a greater sense of ease in the company of both professors and peers.[15]

What Your Students Can Do Now

From their very first semester, your students should begin or continue studying the language of the country they want to study in. If they are heritage learners, they should continue to learn their language formally by taking the highest-level course they test into, and they should complete every course they are able to. If they are starting from the beginner level, they should take as many courses as they can before they graduate. If they come into college and continue a language they had in high school, they should begin by taking the most challenging courses they can get into. Whatever level they are at, they should try to study abroad, either for a semester, a summer, or even a winter break. As mentioned above, language courses are ideal not only because they maintain and accelerate language acquisition but because they enroll fewer students and meet more frequently than most courses, so students can get to know their teachers more readily. These will be among the first teachers they can ask to write their letters of recommendation. If your students are Pell-eligible, then they qualify to apply for the Gilman Scholarship and should do so. If they are studying a non-Romance language, there are a half-dozen significant "critical language" scholarships they can apply for to study the language abroad.

9. EXPERIENCE APPLYING FOR SCHOLARSHIPS

Most students are familiar with the idea that "success breeds success"; that is, that once you have proven you are successful at something, others will assume that you are successful and you will be rewarded with more success. Studies actually demonstrate the validity of this bias, especially early in one's career.[16] This rule tends to hold for success in winning scholarships as well. Once a student has won a scholarship, it's more likely they will succeed when applying for others. Succeeding the first time, however, is difficult, and most of us fail several times before we succeed. Unless a student takes the time to analyze what they might have done better when they fail, they won't be able to apply lessons learned to subsequent scholarship applications. In other words, the secret to getting better at applying for fellowships *is to apply for fellowships*. Just like learning to ride a bike, learning a language, playing an instrument, or learning to dance, the key is, "practice, practice, practice."

As already mentioned, the number, range, and purpose of fellowship opportunities has proliferated over the last two decades—not only nationally but within institutions. Your college is likely to have both merit- and need-based scholarships available (beyond the need-based scholarships available through your financial aid office), from the departmental level to the President's Office. The result of this great expansion of awards, intra-institutionally and nationally, is that there are a great number of fellowships (where the relative odds of winning are good). This has created a system of "building-block" scholarships: smaller awards that allow a student to travel abroad, perform an internship, or participate in some form of public service, for example, where the investment of time is modest, the pay-off is handsome (in that the student has an opportunity they wouldn't have had otherwise), and carries the added benefit of a credential that improves the likelihood that they'll win another award. As a student approaches senior year and begins thinking about post-baccalaureate fellowships and other opportunities, if they have applied to several scholarships already, they'll have important experience to draw upon when they apply to the most prestigious scholarships available and will have greatly enhanced their competitiveness.

What Your Students Can Do Now

Because study abroad scholarships are the most numerous and are awarded on the basis of both financial need and merit, your students' chances of success

WHAT IT TAKES TO BE A SUCCESSFUL APPLICANT

in applying for nationally competitive scholarships are better than many other categories of scholarship. However, they need to plan the timing of their applications carefully to accommodate their need to reach the required level of proficiency at their university for permission to study abroad and to be sure that they have satisfied other academic requirements as well. If they cannot study abroad early in their time in college, they should look first within your college for other opportunities. These days most public universities have endowments that fund special interests or projects for which even first- and second-year students are eligible. These kinds of awards develop the skills they will need to win more exclusive fellowships within their majors as they begin thinking about writing a senior thesis or a capstone. Your office is the optimal starting point not only for helping students get the invaluable experience of applying for scholarships (and ultimately winning them) but making your students aware of the opportunities available to them internally as they move from semester to semester. When you help your students acquire that experience and make the most of their opportunities on your campus, you build and maintain a talent pipeline.

EXERCISES: INVENTORY AND REFLECTION ON INTERESTS, ACTIVITIES, STRENGTHS, AND PRIORITIES

Complete the following exercises. They will help you create an "inventory" of activities and achievements and ask you to reflect on their coherence. List most significant extracurricular activities during college (clubs, organizations, recreation, i.e., student government, Model UN, jazz ensemble, hiking, etc.). But if you are a first- or second-year student, be sure to include activities from high school. Begin with the ones you have performed the longest and that are most meaningful to you. The number of activities on your list may also vary depending on how much time you are required to spend earning income or fulfilling family obligations.

EXTRACURRICULAR AND SERVICE ACTIVITIES

List most significant extracurricular activities during college (e.g., clubs, organizations, recreation, student government, Model UN, jazz ensemble, hiking, etc.).

_____
_____
_____

WHAT IT TAKES TO BE A SUCCESSFUL APPLICANT

_____
_____

List most significant community and public service activities (e.g., soup kitchen, peer counseling, blood bank volunteer, etc.).

_____
_____
_____
_____
_____

REFLECTION ON SOCIAL, CULTURAL, AND POLITICAL INTERESTS

1. How have you chosen and prioritized your activities? Have your activities contributed to your personal or academic growth and development and, if so, how? Which have been the most meaningful or significant, and in what ways?
2. What newspapers/periodicals do you read regularly? What podcasts do you listen to?
3. What are your hobbies and how do you spend your spare time? How long have you been engaged in these pursuits and how often do you engage in them now? How do they relate to your academic or professional endeavors, if at all? What skills and capacities have you developed through them?
4. Please describe a formative, volunteer, community- or public-service experience in which you explain your role, motivations, accomplishments (and failures or disappointments), and why the experience was meaningful to you.

WHAT ARE YOU GOOD AT? WHAT GOOD CAN YOU DO?

List each of the following, as indicated. When you have finished, write a short paragraph describing the accomplishments, recognitions, skills, and personal qualities that overlap. Where there is no overlap, identify areas you would like to develop further or you might "let go of" in the future so that you can devote more time to experiences you now care about more.

Skills

_____
_____

Achievements, prizes, awards

Internships and jobs

Leadership experiences

What are your best qualities (strengths)?

What attributes make you valuable to a group creating something or bringing about a necessary change?

What are your weaknesses?

What skills do you lack that you would like to acquire?

NOTES

1. My friend and colleague is Thomas F. McDow, historian of Africa, the Indian Ocean region, world history, and global health. He joined the faculty at Ohio State in 2011 and was of great help to me developing my summer school personal statement writing course at Hunter.
2. On first-generation academic expectations and help-seeking, see Rachel Gable, "On Academic Experiences," chap. 3 in *The Hidden Curriculum: First Generation Students at Legacy Universities* (Princeton, NJ: Princeton University Press, 2021), and Nicole M. Stephens, MarYam G. Hamedani, and Mesmin Destin, "Closing the Social-Class Achievement Gap: A Difference-Education Intervention Improves First-Generation Students' Academic Performance and All Students' College Transition," *Psychological Science* 25, no. 4 (April 2014): 943–53.
3. Emily Johnson, interview with the author via Zoom, May 8, 2023.
4. Emily's experience mirrors the ideal described by students interviewed for Richard J. Light's book, *Making the Most Out of College: Students Speak Their Minds* (Cambridge, MA: Harvard University Press, 2001), 20–21.
5. Note, I don't elaborate on this aspect of successful applications in this chapter because I devote significant space to it in Chapter 4.
6. Light, *Making the Most Out of College*, 86.
7. See Karna Walter's very helpful essay on this topic, "Involving Faculty in the Scholarship Effort," in *Leading the Way: Student Engagement and Nationally Competitive Awards*, ed. Suzanne McCray (Fayetteville, AK: University of Arkansas Press, 2009), 85–92.
8. Gable, "On Academic Experiences," chap. 3 in *Hidden Curriculum*; see especially p. 90.
9. Those of you familiar with Karna Walter's essay on student engagement will recognize this advice as partaking in the spirit of the "high impact educational practices" adopted by many universities over the past two decades. Many of these practices, however, are out of reach for the majority of students at large public universities or are accessible only to students lucky enough to get good advising early in their college careers. See Karna Walter, "Student Engagement: A Road to Travel More," in *Roads Less Traveled and Other Perspectives on Nationally Competitive Scholarships*, ed. Suzanne McCray and Joanne Brzinski (Fayetteville, AK: University of Arkansas Press, 2017), 53–64.
10. This is a gloss, essentially, on advice about the importance of mentoring that Richard Light gives in various parts of *Making the Most Out of College*, but see especially p. 86.
11. See "Criteria: Leadership Potential," on the website for the Marshall Scholarship, at www.marshallscholarship.org/apply/eligibility/criteria-leadership-potential.
12. Michelle Douenias, Senior Program Manager, Luce Scholars Program at the Henry Luce Foundation, email to the author, June 25, 2023.
13. See the "Frequently Asked Questions" page and the "Leadership Essay" in the sample application (from 2020) on the website for the Schwarzman Scholarship, at www.schwarzmanscholars.org/frequently-asked-questions/, and www.schwarzmanscholars.org/wp-content/uploads/2020/04/Schwarzman-Scholars-Sample-Application-2020.pdf, respectively.
14. We'll discuss this later in Chapter 5.

15. See the testimony of first-generation students at Harvard and Georgetown interviewed by Rachel Gable, *Hidden Curriculum*, 60–70.
16. Arnout van de Rijt, Soong Moon Kang, Michael Restivo, and Akshay Patil, "Field Experiments of Success-Breeds-Success Dynamics," *Proceedings of the National Academy of Sciences of the United States of America* 111, no. 19 (April 28, 2014): 6934–39, https://doi.org/10.1073/pnas.131683611.

WORKS CITED

Gable, Rachel. *The Hidden Curriculum: First Generation Students at Legacy Universities*. Princeton, NJ: Princeton University Press, 2021.

Light, Richard J. *Making the Most Out of College: Students Speak Their Minds*. Cambridge, MA: Harvard University Press, 2001.

Marshall Scholarship. "Criteria: Leadership Potential." www.marshallscholarship.org/apply/eligibility/criteria-leadership-potential.

Schwarzman Scholars. "Frequently Asked Questions." www.schwarzmanscholars.org/frequently-asked-questions/.

Schwarzman Scholars. "Leadership Essay." *2020 Sample Application*. www.schwarzmanscholars.org/wp-content/uploads/2020/04/Schwarzman-Scholars-Sample-Application-2020.pdf.

Stephens, Nicole M., MarYam G. Hamedani, and Mesmin Destin. "Closing the Social-Class Achievement Gap: A Difference-Education Intervention Improves First-Generation Students' Academic Performance and All Students' College Transition." *Psychological Science* 25, no. 4 (April 2014): 943–53.

van de Rijt, Arnout, Soong Moon Kang, Michael Restivo, and Akshay Patil. "Field Experiments of Success-Breeds-Success Dynamics." *Proceedings of the National Academy of Sciences of the United States of America* 111, no. 19 (April 28, 2014): 6934–39, 10.1073/pnas.131683611.

Walter, Karna. "Involving Faculty in the Scholarship Effort." In *Leading the Way: Student Engagement and Nationally Competitive Awards*, edited by Suzanne McCray. Fayetteville, AK: University of Arkansas Press, 2009.

Walter, Karna. "Student Engagement: A Road to Travel More." In *Roads Less Traveled and Other Perspectives on Nationally Competitive Scholarships*, edited by Suzanne McCray and Joanne Brzinski. Fayetteville, AK: University of Arkansas Press, 2017.

Chapter 3

"Who Are You?" Helping Your Students Know Who They Are

Before your students begin writing the personal statement for a fellowship application, very few of them will have had any significant experience writing about themselves. As a form of writing, it feels unnatural. And it's doubly challenging because in some ways the writer has to "stand outside" of themselves while writing about their internal experience. Unlike the personal statement for the college application, which, these days, too often veers into a kind of confessional mode of writing, the centerpiece of the personal statement for a fellowship application is what your student wants to study or achieve: their intellectual mission.[1] While the personal statement should be "personal" in the sense of discussing what a student cares about most, as a genre, it asks the applicant to convey who they are and who they hope to become through the vehicle of the fellowship. A student's most accurate and instructive self-portrayal, then, *might* describe their family members, their neighborhood, their parents' jobs, their religion, obligations to others, and how they spend their time. However, whatever information they choose to disclose must connect directly to their interest in whatever project they intend to carry out during the fellowship. Unlike the personal statement for a college admissions application, it is not about persistence and overcoming adversity. If they choose to roam beyond describing a purely intellectual puzzle to include some aspect of their background and experience, the narrative must connect a specific insight into the phenomena they want to explore, or the course of study they want to pursue. Handled skillfully, your student's personal history can offer the richest, most comprehensible clues to their sensibilities, affiliations, loyalties, dreams, and ambitions. This is because the persuasiveness of their personal statement will rest on the degree to which they are able to elucidate their motives for caring about what they care for and why—whether it is William Shakespeare, Frantz Fanon, making art, or curing cancer.

To help a student arrive at a clearer sense of their motives, you may want to suggest that they complete one of the writing exercises listed below.

> **WRITING EXERCISES FOR YOUR STUDENTS: WHEN DID YOU BECOME "YOU"?**
>
> - Write about a moment from your past, before you left your family's home, when you became conscious of yourself as a distinct person and realized that your destiny would be different from your other family members'—when, in effect, you became "you."
> - Write about a turning point in your life: an event, whether accidental or sought out, that forever changed you or your circumstances. What were the consequences? If you could reverse the event or your decision would you do it? If so, why?
> - Write about a realization that confirmed for you the importance of your personal or political or social obligations to others.

Whatever your student writes about in one of the exercises above may or may not relate directly to what they will write about in their personal statement. But self-understanding (and arising from this, *authenticity*) is the key to what is, at base, a process of developing a narrative about their connection to the world of ideas. What your student writes in any one of these exercises will likely consist of too many words for their personal statement. But it's necessary for a student to be able to articulate for themselves, in an unrestricted fashion, something about their experience that, for them, is essential to who they are or want to become. It may explain their orientation to the world and their desire to address some intellectual question or solve a social, political, or practical problem. In the end, the student will leave behind most of what they wrote for the exercise. In the process of editing their personal statement to get it under the word count, they will be forced to express the most meaningful, pertinent parts of their story, which will anchor the rest of the application.

An idea from the renowned author and writing teacher John McPhee is relevant here. Speaking of something any writer must do—select from all of the material they might include in a piece of writing—McPhee compares the process to grocery shopping for ingredients to make a meal. Once you return from the store, he says, "You set [the ingredients] out on the kitchen counter, and what's there is what you deal with, and all you deal with. If something is red and globular, you don't call it a tomato if it's a bell pepper."[2] The "tomato," "bell pepper," and other ingredients, in your student's case, might be activities, commitments, or accomplishments. Your student needs to select which among these "ingredients" they'll write about—and, as we discussed earlier, connect what they select ("connect the dots"). They need to make clear how the activities, commitments, and accomplishments they choose to write about affirm their underlying sense of purpose and speak to who they are. Can they tether them to the way they were raised or to how they have evolved and come to understand themselves? How do they relate to what they want to do in the future? Ask your students to review the exercise they completed at the end of Chapter 2 about what they're good at and what good they can do in the world. Most student essays about a childhood turning point will involve family members, as they are the primary people in their lives up until and even after college, and thus an important touchstone when they contemplate who they are.

TOUCHSTONES

I know a number of students who have relied on an older sibling for the kind of perspective even a trusted mentor can't provide. Because an older sibling has known a younger sister or brother intimately over a long period of time and has, sometimes, already blazed a professional trail, they recognize when their sibling is being authentic in their self-presentation and may also understand what is wanted by fellowship, admissions, or search committees. Because they have traversed similar terrain academically and developmentally, an older sibling can often be more useful in this regard than a parent, whose own experience may be irrelevant, antiquated, or non-existent. Parents, nonetheless, *do* bear memories that can unlock unnoticed or unquestioned parts of the way the student perceives the world and their place in it.

Because many of my students come from immigrant families, where they come from is often far away. And while these young people have internalized some version of their parents' journeys to the United States, frequently the story they know is a truncated, sanitized version of the twists and turns their parents' lives took between the time they decided to leave their places of birth and arrived in the United States. Often, then, the "known" narrative of their parents' journey obscures difficulties and profound sacrifices. So I always suggest that students interview their parents separately and together, to hear the entire account of their paths and for insight into their parents' and ultimately their own lives. Most of the time, once they learn the whole story of how their parents came to the US, they have a deeper, more refined understanding of their parents' attitudes and beliefs, and thus of their own perspectives and why they differ from or resemble those of their peers.

Yet even if your student's family has been living in the US for generations, they may cling to an assumption that they know well their family's story and where they come from. Most children, however, even after they themselves have grown into young adults, are remarkably incurious about their parents' lives before they became their parents. As children, we learn to accept the world as it is presented to us. As we come to understand our place within our own families, we tend to accept even the most patent contradictions we encounter in the stories we've grown up with about the people perched in parts of our family trees.

This is why an important first step for your students in preparing to apply for a fellowship is to interview their parents about what they remember about their own upbringing, education, where they came of age, their work history, family formation, and where *their* parents came from. If your students' parents are unaccustomed to talking about their feelings and personal experiences and seem resistant to the idea of speaking about them, an ideal place for them to begin the conversation is to ask their parents about their work lives.[3] Beginning their conversation with questions about something as concrete as their jobs can dissolve any awkwardness and yield some arresting discoveries, probably more empathy for their parents, and with reflection, greater self-understanding for the student. Surprises are inevitably revealed—some relevant to the student's emerging understanding of themselves, some incidental and insignificant. But interviewing their parents almost always yields new insights into their own motives, a vision of who they want to be and why.

Larisa, a student I worked with several years ago who went on to Harvard Medical School, interviewed her mother about her reasons for immigrating to the United States so she could understand her own smoldering desire to "make something of herself." Interviewing her mother gave Larisa a view into her parents' decision to leave the former Soviet Union, what they lost and left behind when they emigrated, and what uprooting their lives meant to them and how it shaped their hopes for their daughter. These expectations were even more freighted by the fact that Larisa's father eventually died from a prolonged illness after they immigrated. However, learning about her parents' dreams and their reflection on the meaning of the circumstances that had formed them clarified for Larisa the choices her parents had made in raising her. In the excerpt below, Larisa's story illustrates the power of exploring the connections between one's family's history and one's own drives and emerging sense of self:

> My parents raised me to never take my American status for granted, but also not to forget my mother tongue, Russian, and the region of Russia in which I was born, the Caucasus. However, as a child, I always felt as though being a Russian immigrant isolated me from making American friends. Everything was different about me—the way I spoke, the way I dressed and even what I ate for lunch. Mortified by my last name ["Shagabayeva"], I worried that it was too difficult sounding to be "American," as school friends and teachers butchered its pronunciation. I became embarrassed to speak Russian and started to forget the language altogether. ... My parents didn't observe the Sabbath or maintain kosher laws, so it was difficult to invite school friends to our home without fear of judgment. I knew nothing of my background,

except that I was different—and I hated it ... Although I never got an adequate explanation for why my parents sent me to a yeshivah, I imagine it was an act of defiance in which my parents re-asserted their identities as Jews in a country that allowed them to do so. Years of propaganda against religion in the Soviet Union were hard to undo and were very much evident in their responses to my Jewish education, but a revival of Jewish identity, at least culturally, for all of us was promised through my yeshivah education. However, I also realized that despite experiencing anti-Semitism in the Soviet Union, my parents found it important to preserve [their] culture, as evidenced by its strong presence in our home. Juggling dual identities as a Russian Jewish refugee and American citizen was often difficult, but, with better understanding of my background, I was able to merge these two and practice a single identity of a New American. To me, this meant celebrating American principles of religious freedom and respect for overall diversity from the perspective of a refugee, and it also meant honoring adversity and strength in the immigrant story. My mother's dream was realized through the achievement of my own dreams when I was accepted to Harvard Medical School, something that may have never been possible if she hadn't made the sacrifice to leave Russia. All the hardships that came about with immigration like serious financial struggles, language and cultural barriers, and the overall trauma of leaving one's home out of desperation were endured by my parents to provide me with opportunity. I was inspired by my parents' resilience as refugees and was honored to realize that what seemed to be my accomplishment also became my parents' and encouragement for other immigrants and refugees as well.[4]

Learning the details of her parents' sacrifices helped Larisa understand not only their life-altering decisions but less momentous if still formative choices about her own schooling, as well as her relationship to her parents' cultural background and origins. In other words, it gave her insight into herself, which enabled her to "situate" her own values and posture toward the world.

*

Interviewing parents, then, can unearth previously unappreciated opportunities for self-comprehension. Similarly, taking the time to narrate one's own life brings other understandings into focus as one considers the ways that the stories we tell others (and ourselves) about ourselves may unwittingly determine the choices we make. I'm reminded here of Robert Steven Kaplan's urging his students, advisees, and readers to write down the stories of their lives, as a first step toward self-knowledge.[5] Kaplan's purpose is to help his students think about what drives and impedes them; what situations or kinds of people pose problems for them and why. Writing out a narrative of our lives, he argues, helps us to apprehend the role of others in constructing who we are, what spurs or inhibits us, and why we make the decisions we do. As Kaplan demonstrates through the example of his own parents' biographies and their effect on him, much of what inspires him, causes him worry, and even shapes his goals, can be traced back to what he experienced as their son. There is no finger-pointing here. His aim in this exercise—for himself and for his readers—is not to blame anyone for the choices or mistakes he or they have made. Rather, his aim in urging us to follow his example is for us to *become aware* of why we do what we do. I suggest that you encourage your advisees to read his chapter, "Understanding Yourself," from his book *What You're Really Meant to Do*. But let me briefly outline his main points for you here and ask that you try his exercise first, because this will help you understand the kinds of discoveries your students may uncover for themselves.

After writing down your "basic story," as he calls it, what themes do you notice?[6] What issues are important, either articulated or subliminal in your upbringing? Was money (for example) a recurrent issue when you were growing up? Were rules and conforming important? Were there different standards for girls and boys in your family? Were you conscious of this and if so, how did you feel about it? How were success and failure measured and were there exemplars of each type in your extended family?

Kaplan's key piece of advice is that his students/readers think about three different kinds of narratives that they carry around within them: "success narratives," "failure narratives," and "injustice narratives." He asks his students to write each of these down. Success narratives are stories that describe an ideal version of oneself, without faults and stumbles. Stripped away are self-doubt and perhaps even the amount of work it took to accomplish the things the writer is proud of. Success narratives help us believe in ourselves and give us the confidence we need to strive toward goals that may seem beyond our reach. Even while we know they are not the whole truth, they serve a very useful purpose.

A failure narrative is the job interview your student flubbed, the organic chemistry course they failed, a time they let a friend or loved one down, or self-defeating behaviors that prevent them from being at their best: anxious thoughts, for instance, that inhibit them from connecting with others, or feigned self-confidence, which dissuades them from asking for help. Most of us keep these narratives buried as we move through our lives. It may be healthy to some extent to do so to keep from being paralyzed by fear that we'll succumb to them. However, Kaplan persuades us that becoming aware of what he calls the "competing narratives" we carry around enables us to explain our behavior to ourselves and to understand the choices we make—choices that may, in fact, be getting in the way of doing things necessary to fulfill our potential.

The third type of narrative that Kaplan considers is the injustice narrative. Kaplan points out that most of us have experienced *some* form of injustice during our lives; that is, some situation in which we were wronged for no apparent reason—passed over for recognition, unfairly dismissed, or even demonstrably discriminated against. It's just as important, he says, to come to terms with slights, large and small, because they may play into our conception of our abilities and potential. Just as a failure narrative can silently inform the way we approach opportunities (or avoid them), an injustice narrative can unconsciously cause us to self-discourage, withdraw from others, or behave defensively. Part of whatever imposter syndrome we may experience (which many of us do) may stem from unfair treatment. Kaplan urges us to compose our narratives of injustice, take them apart, diagnose them, and come to terms with what kind of ongoing influence they may be having on us. These three narratives continually contend with one another—success narratives on one side, failure and injustice narratives on the other—to form "competing narratives," which persist in the recesses of the psyche unexamined.

"Once you've written these narratives," he says, "think about the circumstances under which each of them is in your head."

> Is it possible that, when you made a good or a confident decision, the success narrative was in your head? Conversely, has your failure narrative kept you from speaking up at work or asserting yourself in critical situations? ... The challenge isn't about getting rid of it or morphing it into another kind of thought. Instead, the challenge is to figure out how our narratives are impacting our behaviors—and in particular, how and why they're holding us back. Is it justified, or only an old and unproductive relic of a previous phase of your life?[7]

For many students, subconscious factors can affect the way they approach any opportunity, calculating the effort they would need to put into an application versus the odds of winning it. Of course, we all do this to some degree. But students often operate with incomplete or distorted information about fellowship opportunities, especially at institutions like mine, where the very concept is so foreign. Frequently, when I ask students if they have considered applying for a particular scholarship they demur and reply, "But isn't it *really* competitive?" I tell them that of course it is, but this shouldn't dissuade them from considering applying. And this is where it's useful for them to think about the narratives that Kaplan talks about. What sorts of obstacles are they placing in their own paths before they even contemplate applying? Do their failure narratives or injustice narratives engender self-discouragement before they even think about what an opportunity could do for them?

Composing a personal statement forces the writer to make explicit their dreams and to articulate their purpose. Dreams are usually easier to verbalize than a sense of purpose. There are lots of examples walking around of the kind of person your students might imagine becoming. Defining one's sense of purpose is the hard part. That is, what we derive satisfaction from, why, and how it benefits others. Kaplan's book also talks helpfully about finding one's path, but the key issue for your students in recording and analyzing their narratives is to understand how they "frame" themselves internally, because this informs both their dreams and the obstacles they erect that prevent them from fulfilling their dreams.

Applying for a fellowship operationalizes the process Kaplan describes because, whereas examining their competing narratives helps the applicant understand themselves to make better-informed future decisions, applying for a fellowship asks the writer to distill their introspection into a plan of action. Describing their strengths, interests, and aptitudes and connecting these to an intellectual mission, despite their internal competing narratives, forces a student to externalize what's possible and to persuade others that they are uniquely positioned to follow through on what they propose to do.

Nevertheless, plumbing their past, as Kaplan suggests, and understanding where they come from and how where they're going relates to who they are, is a necessary first step for students to take before they write their personal statements. By surrounding themselves with people they trust to "hold the mirror up" to their accomplishments and aspirations, they can begin to assemble all the parts of their lives into a coherent whole. Mentors, too, whether they are teachers, advisors, or intimates who are closer in age, can help your students begin to formulate personal statements about who they are and where they come from that put them on a path to fulfilling their purpose. Intrinsically, the personal statement gives them a way of understanding themselves—however contingent—that will remind them of their purpose and sustain them in moments of self-doubt and feelings of directionlessness. When a student offers a fellowship committee a coherent account of who they are and how they came to care about what they propose to study, it makes them vivid as a candidate and enhances their odds of winning the scholarship they're applying for.

IMPOSTER SYNDROME AND SELF-DISCOURAGEMENT

Kaplan's failure and injustice narratives are close cousins of imposter syndrome. The inverse of who your students are and hope to be is who they are *not* and who they fear they will never become. At each of the schools I worked at previously there was an abundance of students sufficiently self-possessed to put themselves forward as credible candidates for the most competitive fellowships. Over the last two decades some of the most renowned fellowships have restricted the number of applicants each institution can endorse or nominate so that fellowship committees can manage the volume of applications they receive.[8] But at the private institutions I worked at, I found, students from historically underrepresented groups routinely underestimated their ability to compete and tended to "self-discourage" early in their college careers.[9] Thus, they were rarely in a position to apply for major post-baccalaureate fellowships as they approached graduation. Similarly, in my subsequent experience at a large urban public university, the great majority of students—regardless of their social or ethnic background—commonly express feelings of being underprepared and "unworthy."[10] Precisely because they aren't enrolled at a highly selective institution, students like these "self-discourage" in the sense of failing to consider themselves competitive simply because their college is not among the most selective in the land. (Enough of them, moreover, have friends, former classmates, or even siblings at highly selective universities to routinely reinforce the sense that they "don't measure up.") The challenge for those of us at large public universities, then, is to make our students aware of opportunities early in their college careers and equip them to be credible candidates for major fellowships in the future.

Whether you work at a private college or at a large public university, your students' insecurities—even their endearing sense of modesty—may cause them to overestimate the abilities and accomplishments of everyone around them and to undervalue themselves. Just as it can be difficult for them to judge others accurately, it's often difficult for them to gain the full measure of themselves. What is more, they are at an age when they are particularly prone to comparing themselves with others in every respect. Beside their classmates they may often feel diminished. Too often they don't dare to imagine what they might be capable of achieving because parents teach them about hard work, perseverance, and habits of mind that lead to reliable careers along known, rutted professional pathways. Maybe they had the good fortune of being accepted at a number of highly ranked institutions when they applied to college, but their parents felt they couldn't afford the expense of a pricey university. Or perhaps their parents never finished college themselves and know that it's important for their child to complete their degree but regard it solely as a means to an end—a necessity—rather than the obsession it has become for your student, which may now include graduate school. Understanding that singular goal, what drives your student, is central to understanding who they are.

My students, collectively, reflect the social and cultural complexity of the world's most linguistically diverse metropolitan area. Many of their parents make modest incomes. Many of *their* parents didn't finish secondary school and speak little or no English. Some of my students' parents worked as doctors or engineers before emigrating to the United States, but as is all too common, were locked out of the careers they had embarked on in the communities they left behind. Because they wanted to create better lives for their children, they took what they could find in their adopted country: work that is sometimes (but often not) related to, but much less remunerative than, what they had trained to do for a living. Many of my students speak two and sometimes even three or four languages. Many of them come from families in which they are constantly compared to a high-achieving sister or brother; or even more burdensome, they represent their family's best hope to succeed in America and therefore to validate their parents' decision to leave their country of birth.

Because my students are peaking cognitively during a time when they're also being exposed to worlds of new information and novel concepts, I *expect* to learn about their blossoming intellectual interests. But it is what I come to know about the other parts of their lives that I find so astonishing: a 20-hour-a-week job, a chronically ill or disabled family member, an uncomprehending parent, the student's lengthy commute to school, the sacrifices their parents made to come to the United States, the student's role as family translator, the number of jobs their parents work, the family's constant fear of being deported, a nagging awareness of what the student "owes" to others, and finally, their family's insistence that they spin flax into gold with their college degree. Beneath all of this is the peptic coexistence of humility and ambition churning within. It would be understandable if they experienced any one of these things as immobilizing. To a reader of fellowship applications, their stories are at once sobering and inspiring. What each of us is apt to take for granted about ourselves is often beyond our inclination to consider when we are taking stock of what will positively impress a fellowship committee. In short, students need to be encouraged *not* to take for granted what is remarkable about themselves.

Imposter syndrome—the feeling of "phoniness in people who believe that they are not intelligent, capable or creative despite evidence of high achievement"—has become such a commonplace that even the most accomplished people admit to feelings of fraudulence.[11] Another phrase linked to the feeling that we're all imposters until we're not is "fake it till you make it," the mantra of Silicon Valley. Silicon Valley is apparently filled with young professionals working for nothing and in obscurity until they get their big break. But for many, "faking it" is a luxury only the financially comfortable can afford. Most of my students can't afford to gamble on a big bet that they don't *know* will pay off. They need a predictable, secure path more than the chance to make a fortune. On one hand, it should be comforting to know that even very successful people are wracked by insecurity until they prove themselves. On the other hand, if they come from a family in which there is no one who has already proven they can finish college, it's hard for them to feel confident that they will not only graduate but go on to distinguish themselves in the world of fellowship competitions as well.

Yes, self-confidence is important, but more important is authenticity. Authenticity is the key to writing a powerful personal statement, which we will discuss in Chapter 5, but a student's *authentically* coming to terms with feelings that they don't belong—to a fellowship or the graduate school that admitted them or a desirable internship—is important if they are going to perform at the level that made the opportunity possible in the first place. A student I've advised for several years recently ruminated on her experience of imposter syndrome, concluding pithily about her own worries of unworthiness that, "feelings are not facts." "Feeling like you don't belong," she observed, "doesn't mean that you don't in fact belong." This is someone who was a finalist for a major national fellowship. Crushed by her disappointment when she didn't win, she nonetheless went on to gain admission to a top law school and won a major fellowship for women pursuing careers in law. Even so, self-doubt gnaws at her from time to time. In her more buoyant moments, she says,

> I was able to wear my differences with pride as something like a badge of honor, fully aware of how much harder it was for me to have made it to [law school] in the first place ... on the tougher days I struggled to see myself as deserving of a spot in my graduate program, especially when compared to my well-resourced peers, who seemed to be navigating every challenge that was thrown their way with ease.[12]

Ultimately, she realized that remembering where she comes from fuels the work she hopes to do one day with a law degree from such a highly regarded institution, so she revisits familiar touchstones to remind herself of her mission.

For our students, transcending the feeling that they "don't belong," which is, fundamentally, what imposter syndrome is about—the feeling that *they* are fake but everyone around them deserves to belong—is their first task on the way to becoming who they will be: acknowledging their feelings but then embracing the fact that they were among those chosen for the opportunity they now enjoy. Being their authentic selves will ensure that they make good decisions, communicate better, build trust with others, and work more effectively. They shouldn't assume that they will impress people more and be more appealing by pretending they're someone else. If people know that the person they see and hear is who they really are, they will be judged more fairly and their ideas are likely to be better received.

College is a time in students' lives when they are working hard to understand who they are and are only beginning to glimpse who they might become. College, moreover, affords a student the developmental and (often) the physical space to establish themselves as an individual, distinct from their families and the communities they grew up in. Also, getting a college education—especially if a student is the first person in their family's history to attend college—is in its way an act of self-transcendence: many of them are, consciously or not, working to supersede their family's traditions or, at the very least, their economic disadvantage, and perhaps even some of the values they espouse, in exchange for new ways of seeing and experiencing the world, as well as the kinds of opportunities only available to someone with a college degree. This act of self-transcendence, however, can feel to some students like a form of *self*-betrayal too, and so while the ideas students encounter in college and the possibilities that await them afterward may be exhilarating, the experience can be fraught with ambivalence. Paradoxically, these same students, even as they strive to differentiate themselves from others, tend to think of themselves as too ordinary. That is, too much like everyone they've grown up with to be considered competitive for scholarships.

What if your student comes from less dramatic circumstances? While many of their classmates are anxious to fit in and to be normal in the sense of acting and feeling as "American" or middle class as their age peers, your student may come from the suburbs or the exurbs of Long Island, rural Ohio, Arizona, or Colorado and might, consequently, feel pejoratively "average" in a different way. Perhaps they've had the benefit of an unblemished childhood, grew up with play dates, organized sports, family vacations, excelled academically and extracurricularly through high school. They set their sights on college without knowing or even imagining what worlds lay beyond what members of their own family do for a living, where they went to college.

Sitting as they do at the center of what makes them who they are actually hampers their ability to make sense of themselves—to perceive connections between the parts and the whole.[13] If the point of the personal statement is to demonstrate how unique and well-suited they are for the fellowships they're applying for, how can they know what is noteworthy and relevant about aspects of themselves they can't even see? I will bang on this drum again: by *seeking out mentors*. But whether their mentor is a professor, coach, or community service director, because they are older, more experienced, and observe so many students over time, they are positioned to know what your students have in common with their peers and what sets them apart. Your students usually can't see what's extraordinary about themselves because they live with, endure, and overcome challenges, responsibilities, and disadvantages simply because *they must*. A mentor can.

Still, in the end, it falls to your students to describe what distinguishes them from other applicants and to do so with all the grace they muster to manage the daily complications of their lives. They are the only ones who can show fellowship application readers how the parts of their lives relate to the *whole person*. The collection of experiences they've have had, intentionally or not, the roles they have undertaken, jobs, internships, clubs, hobbies, and talents they have cultivated through sports, music, theater, or dance, and their commitments, to a religion perhaps, caring for a family member, or some form of volunteer work—all together—provide the elements they need to create their stories.

Who we appear to be, it's important to remember, governs the way most people see us. The résumé presents a version of your student that places them among other similarly successful young people as they apply for fellowships or graduate school. But after a committee's first round of readings, the information on that document itself may not sufficiently separate them from others that selection committees will seriously consider. What will make your students stand out is what they say about themselves in their personal statements: who they are, how they think, what interests them and why, and how it is that they have been drawn to study world migration, Homer, human trafficking, or Flemish painting.

Before they begin the process of presenting themselves, it can be helpful to contemplate the apparent contradictions that they live with but rarely consider. They might start with the discontinuities between their success narratives and failure narratives. Both are versions of the truth but also partial truths. They combine to make your student who they are, but these narratives may also be at war within them without their even realizing it. In the end, of course, the personal statement will offer its own success narrative because, after all, the point is to demonstrate their worthiness, not their vulnerabilities. Moreover, just because they have also suffered failures doesn't invalidate their successes or ability to carry out the goal of the fellowship they're applying for. The kind of introspection Kaplan prescribes will enable them to understand what motivates them. Their motives, in turn, will help them get at the most effective way to present their authentic selves. Authenticity, whether their lives have been filled with difficulty or appear to others as sheltered and even uninteresting, is the key to presenting a persuasive vision of what they hope to accomplish and why it matters.

EXERCISE: INTERVIEWING PARENTS

Most people don't know as much about their parents as they believe they do. Often their sense of chronology is wrong, as well as their understanding of where their parents lived, where they went to school, what their motives were at critical decision points, and so on. Usually, we carry around some sanitized version of the lives our parents have led, because it's natural for parents not to discuss with their children the more painful (and mundane) parts of their experience. Their misfortunes, the nature of their relations with other family members, attitudes toward people who are not like them, religion, politics, and so on are often only dimly understood and rarely pursued. The questions below will help you document the most basic facts about your parents as well as fill in some more meaningful details. This exercise can lead to further, more in-depth conversations and greater empathy for your parents and understanding of yourself. If at all possible, you should record this, with your parents' permission.

QUESTIONS FOR INTERVIEWS WITH PARENTS

Interview your parents separately. Before beginning, record their full names, and when and where they were they born. (Note, these are questions as posed to parents.)

Grandparents (and Immigration)

How did *your* parents meet and decide to get married? How many children did they have?

What type of work did/do they do?

If they immigrated to the US, what do they remember about the journey? Are there any notable family stories about the journey?

What was most difficult about their transition to living in the United States?

Childhood

How many siblings did you have? Record their number and birth order.

Can you talk about an early (or favorite) memory of each of your siblings?

What do you remember about any of your friends from early childhood?

Middle Childhood and Adolescence (Years 6–18)

What do you remember about your neighborhood visually or physically? Did you move very much when you were growing up? How many different places did you live? Do you know why you moved each time?

Did you or any of your siblings have your own rooms? At what age did you get your own room?

Who was your best friend when you were growing up? What do you remember about them?

How did you spend your time outside of school and outside of organized activities as you moved through grade school, then high school?

Did you play any organized sports growing up? Which ones? What were your favorites?

Did your family have dinner together most nights? What do you remember about them?

Who was the primary cook in your household? Who cleaned up after meals?

Did you regularly do household chores growing up? How were these tasks divided?

How often did you get new clothes? Did you feel as well-dressed as your peers when growing up?

Did your family ever take any vacations? Where did you go? What was your favorite?

What sort of entertainment did you like? (Music? Movies? Television?)

Schooling

How many schools did you attend before college and where were they?

What was a favorite memory from grade school?

Did you like high school? What were your favorite and least favorite parts of high school?

What subjects did you like, and why?

Did you have any favorite teachers?

How did gender roles affect you between grade school and high school?

How did your awareness of your own and others' race, ethnicity, or social status make you feel about yourself and your friends?

If one or both of your parents attended college: How did you decide where to go to college?

What was your major? Do you feel that your choice of major affected your career choice?

Did you have any influential mentors?

Dating and Marriage

Where and how did you and (mother/father) meet? When did you know that they were the person you wanted to marry?

How long did you date before getting married?

What do you remember from your early relationship?

How old were you when you had your first child?

Career

What did you want to become when you were growing up?

What was your first job?

How much money did you earn in your first job? Did you have to take that job or were you given a choice? How long did you have that job?

How did you choose your career and what is your favorite part about it?

How do you account for the success you've had at work?

Parenting and Family Life

Did you know that you wanted to have children when you got married?

Did you worry about the responsibility of being a parent?

How would you describe your approach to parenting?

Religion/Spirituality/Personal Philosophy

If your parent/parents practice a religion: How do you think about your religion and the role it plays in your life?

If your parent/parents do not practice religion: When did you stop practicing your religion? If so, what caused you to stop?

What is most important to you in life?

Can you point to any particular events that have shaped your life?

What makes you happiest?

How do you want to be remembered?

What are the best decisions you ever made?

Do you have any profound regrets?

NOTES

1. See, e.g., Elijah Megginson, "When I Applied to College, I Didn't Want to 'Sell My Pain,'" *New York Times*, May 9, 2021, www.nytimes.com/2021/05/09/opinion/college-admissions-essays-trauma.html. Note that, in 2022, the Rhodes Scholarship moved away from the personal statement format because it concluded that "over time, personal statements have become increasingly formulaic—and that, particularly over the past 10–15 years, a genre of pathos has emerged with a growing number of personal statements focused on 'overcoming' obstacles or trauma, or on a heroic narrative of problem-solving." My advice here, admittedly, may be less relevant for Rhodes' "reframing," but I maintain that in the process of learning how to write an effective personal statement your students can get much closer to knowing what they want out of the fellowships they apply for and understand themselves much better for having done so. See Elliot Gerson, "Reframing the Rhodes Scholarship Personal Statement," available at https://honorscarolina.unc.edu/wp-content/uploads/2022/05/Rhodes-Trust-New-Personal-Statement-Guidance-1.pdf.
2. John McPhee, "Structure," *New Yorker*, January 14, 2013, 48.

3. Even if their parents perform highly recognizable, seemingly straightforward jobs as teachers, lawyers, or home-health workers, students often have only the faintest idea what their parents *actually do* at work.
4. Larisa Shagabayeva, personal statement, draft 1, September 5, 2018.
5. Robert Steven Kaplan, "Understanding Yourself: The Power of Narrative," chap. 4 in *What You're Really Meant to Do: A Roadmap for Reaching Your Unique Potential* (Boston, MA: Harvard Business Review Publishing, 2012).
6. By "basic story," Kaplan means: where you were born; a description of your parents, siblings, where they live, people they know/knew; and in chronological order, an account of "specific and meaningful experiences" you have had and "incidents at school," as well as "key interactions [with] parents." You should "carry this story right up to the present." See Kaplan, *What You're Really Meant to Do*, 85.
7. Kaplan, *What You're Really Meant to Do*, 93–94, 97.
8. The Luce Scholarship recently reversed this trend, ending its institutional partnerships and opening up its admissions process to create a more diverse applicant pool.
9. This impression—admittedly anecdotal—was formed during my work with more than 2,000 students over a period of twenty years. So far as I know, there is no systematic study of this phenomenon.
10. I benefitted, while contemplating this discussion, from Brandy Simula's essay, "Belonging, Imposter Phenomenon, and Advising Students from Underrpresented Backgrounds," in *Roads Less Traveled and Other Perspectives on Nationally Competitive Scholarships*, ed. Suzanne McCray and Joanne Brzinski (Fayetteville, AK: University of Arkansas Press, 2017), 121–34. And see the brilliant op-ed by Romanian-born author, Costica Bradatan, "I Know What Savage Fear Really Lies at the Heart of the American Dream," *New York Times*, January 2, 2023, www.nytimes.com/2023/01/02/opinion/failure-romania-america.html.
11. Quoted in Carl Richards, "Learning to Deal with Imposter Syndrome," *New York Times*, October 26, 2015, www.nytimes.com/2015/10/26/your-money/learning-to-deal-with-the-impostor-syndrome.html.
12. Anonymous participant in Zoom panel discussion sponsored by my office at Hunter College, January 12, 2022, "Fake It Till You Make It? Unmasking Imposter Syndrome." See also Stacey Abrams's parallel account of her disappointment at not winning the Rhodes, which appears in her introduction to *Minority Leader: How to Lead from the Outside and Make Real Change* (New York: Henry Holt, 2018).
13. The importance of seeing how the parts relate to the whole comes from Richard J. Light, *Making the Most Out of College* (Cambridge, MA: Harvard University Press, 2001), chaps. 2, 5, and 6.

WORKS CITED

Abrams, Stacey. Introduction to *Minority Leader: How to Lead from the Outside and Make Real Change*. New York: Henry Holt, 2018.

Bradatan, Costica. "I Know What Savage Fear Really Lies at the Heart of the American Dream." *New York Times*, January 2, 2023. www.nytimes.com/2023/01/02/opinion/failure-romania-america.html.

Gerson, Elliot. "Reframing the Rhodes Scholarship Personal Statement," May 2022. https://honorscarolina.unc.edu/wp-content/uploads/2022/05/Rhodes-Trust-New-Personal-Statement-Guidance-1.pdf.

Kaplan, Robert Steven. *What You're Really Meant to Do: A Roadmap for Reaching Your Unique Potential.* Boston, MA: Harvard Business Review Publishing, 2012.

Light Richard J. *Making the Most Out of College: Students Speak Their Minds.* Cambridge, MA: Harvard University Press, 2001.

McPhee, John. "Structure." *New Yorker*, January 14, 2013, 46–55.

Megginson, Elijah. "When I Applied to College, I Didn't Want to 'Sell My Pain.'" *New York Times*, May 9, 2021. www.nytimes.com/2021/05/09/opinion/college-admissions-essays-trauma.html.

Richards, Carl. "Learning to Deal with Imposter Syndrome." *New York Times*, October 26, 2015. www.nytimes.com/2015/10/26/your-money/learning-to-deal-with-the-impostor-syndrome.html.

Simula, Brandy. "Belonging, Imposter Phenomenon, and Advising Students from Underrpresented Backgrounds." In *Roads Less Traveled and Other Perspectives on Nationally Competitive Scholarships.* Edited by Suzanne McCray and Joanne Brzinski. Fayetteville, AK: University of Arkansas Press, 2017.

Chapter 4

What a Fellowship Committee Wants to Know about Your Student: Helping Your Students Understand How to Present Themselves

Your students' goal in composing their fellowship applications is to identify patterns in their interests, choices, and competencies and to make sense of the whole for their readers. A coherent presentation of who they are and what they want to accomplish enables them to make the best case for themselves, transforming a faceless applicant into memorable candidate. In Chapter 3 we discussed the importance of helping your students understand themselves, their aims, and purpose. This chapter will discuss the importance of their stepping back to contemplate how their commitments relate to one another.

Figure 4.1 Daniel Hickey, Ossining, NY, 2023. Photograph courtesy of Daniel Hickey

WHAT A FELLOWSHIP COMMITTEE WANTS TO KNOW

For his Fulbright English Teaching Assistant application, Daniel Hickey, one of my fellowship-advisees, in his senior year at the time and still formulating his career plans, wrote about teaching rock climbing. I knew from reading his application essays that he was unusually thoughtful, a very capable writer, and highly proficient in both Arabic and Spanish, so I asked him why he had chosen to write about rock climbing for his personal statement. He said the topic allowed him to talk about overcoming a teaching challenge, which the Fulbright encourages, but also because he had, as a teenager, once considered rock climbing professionally, and the sport had been formative for him as a young person. Realizing at some point in his late teens that he would never reach the level of professional competitors, he abandoned his ambition and resigned himself to climbing recreationally. But he loved the sport so much that he later decided to dedicate himself to teaching younger climbers instead.

When I asked him what he found so appealing about the sport, he said that it shares important qualities with other similarly absorbing activities that require skill, discipline, creativity, and effort: writing and learning other languages. Each of them, he observed,

> poses a challenge that I know I'll get something out of—a sense of accomplishment. Every climb is a problem to solve and like other problems, such as writing a long essay or learning a language, it requires study, practice, repetition, some imagination, and breaking the problem down into its constituent parts ... There's a concept in climbing that we call "linkage." It refers to linking up the sequential parts of a long climb. The other part of completing a climb in "one go" is endurance, so once you have mastered the parts of the climb you have to have the endurance to "link them up," in order to finish it. Both writing a long essay and learning a language are like this. I can turn a nice phrase while writing an essay but that's not the same as writing a whole essay. I can (and do need to) learn more vocabulary to be able to communicate more fully and fluently in Spanish or Arabic, but I need many more of those smaller "parts" to create a nuanced flow of speech in the manner of native speaker of another language.[1]

If your student reflects for a moment on the exercise they performed at the end of Chapter 3, when they "connected the dots" among their activities, interests, and experiences, they may understand it as analogous to the kind of "linkage" that Daniel describes when he masters a climb from beginning to end. Conceiving of accomplishments, interests, and experiences like "holds" on the face of a climbing wall, which when grasped sequentially allow the climber to reach the summit, helpfully underlines the importance of connecting the dots when writing the personal statement.

Once Daniel had identified some themes among his chief forms of satisfaction and joined them together in his personal statement, he had created, in effect, a map for a personal statement that he could use for many different purposes in the future. When he applies for another major fellowship (or graduate school) he can compose an essay that weaves these themes together with an intellectual mission and the goals of the fellowship. In the meantime, he has identified some important qualities in work and play that resonate meaningfully with every one of his significant intellectual and physical endeavors. Together they offer an important clue to what motivates him and this will be the key to envisioning his future.

Alice Tsai, another student I worked with, who was applying to medical school, contemplated a number of experiences she had had beginning as a child. Her parents, who were immigrants from Taiwan, had encouraged her from an early age to perform community service at a Buddhist relief organization. This exposed her to an older generation of people who spoke her parents' language and ultimately inspired her to learn Mandarin formally when she began college. Once she started shadowing doctors in a hospital to meet one of her requirements for applying to medical school, she came to understand the importance of communicating with patients in their own language and appreciated how an empathic healthcare worker could elicit trust and, in turn, information key to their patients' health. Some of her interests were instilled by her parents' wishes (volunteering and learning their native language), others she gravitated toward out of cultural curiosity, and still others were required by her pre-med program. The point is that experiences that give an applicant direction and momentum may appear unrelated and even random to a student until they consider how they might be related. Once this happens, they can begin to compose a narrative that gives shape and meaning to their life and renders their commitments sensible to anyone reading it.[2]

The most successful personal statement explains how the applicant, their activities, their proposed project, and their ambitions match the fellowship's mission. Qualifying is not sufficient. In a crowded pool of candidates, "the person" needs to stand out, and the best way for an applicant to do that is by showing how they choose to spend their time and what they have learned by engaging in those activities. Their interests, skills, aptitudes, commitments, ideals, jobs, goals, preparation, and ultimately their *purpose* elevate them into the handful of candidates being considered. As I will explain in the next chapter, the heart of the personal statement is the intellectual mission your student brings to bear on the fellowship—their reason for needing the support the fellowship provides. But the *connection* between who they are as a person and what they want to study or what project they hope to carry out is what will make them memorable to a selection committee.

By connecting the dots for their readers, their application makes them the candidate the fellowship is looking for—someone who fulfills the selection committee's idea of the kind of person who embodies its purpose. Someone whose involvement in the fellowship and legacy thereafter will be a credit to the organization that bestows it. For the student, connecting the dots for others helps them better understand themselves, to appreciate the larger patterns at work in everything they've been doing. This kind of reflection can energize their own sense of purpose and give them renewed direction and momentum.

SITUATING THEMSELVES

One of the most difficult aspects of writing a personal statement is that the writer must become clear about what they assume others know about them; simply because their own qualities and experiences are so much a part of them that they don't even realize that they require explanation. The first step is making the things they take for granted about themselves *visible to themselves*. The second part is not merely making them visible to others by naming them ("telling") but illustrating for their readers, through vignettes or anecdotes, how they see the world and themselves in it—in other words, "showing." Showing makes the applicant visible and comprehensible to their readers. Here is where the words your student chooses are especially important. And here is one of the differences between a personal statement for a fellowship, where usually the readers are generalists, and a graduate school application, where the readers are specialists. Specialists speak the writer's language and expect them to demonstrate their familiarity with the discourse in their field. Using the rhetoric commonly employed in the literature of the field shows that an applicant is conversant with the latest debates in their discipline and is able to join in the conversation.

There are cases where the readers of fellowship applications are specialists. Science scholarships like the Goldwater or the National Science Foundation Graduate Research Fellowship, for instance, are obviously going to staff their committees primarily with scientists, even if they're not experts in the student's subdiscipline. But there is another genre of fellowships whose readers are specialists in the sense of being particularly attuned to the nuances of social and cultural identity, like scholarships dedicated to increasing opportunities for students from underrepresented backgrounds: students of color, nonbinary students, students whose parents didn't attend college, or whose family income is modest. A growing list of such fellowships that seek to nurture talented thinkers and leaders-in-the-making includes: the AANAPISI Scholarship, the Davis-Putter Scholarship, Emerging Leaders in Public Service, Govern For America, the Institute for Recruitment of Teachers, the Marshall-Motley Scholars Program, the Mellon Mays Undergraduate Fellowship, The Pauli Murray Fellowship, Point Scholarships, the Public Policy and International Affairs Summer Institute, the Paul & Daisy Soros Fellowship, and the When There Are Nine Scholarship. While they vary widely by subject area and intended audience, the shared mission of these fellowships is to develop a more diverse cohort of future leaders in American society. The eligibility criteria for each of them specify membership in or identification with groups historically underrepresented in leadership roles.

If a fellowship describes your student or their aspirations, then they may be a promising candidate. Your student can assume that their readers will view them through a familiar and receptive lens and are acquainted with the concepts and discourse of the student's field of study or orientation. As identity and its valences are the focus of the scholarships listed above, putting the student's identity at the center of their personal statement is not just necessary but desirable. Your student should look to the language on the fellowship's website for ways to describe themselves and their goals in the personal statement and statement of purpose. The essay prompts for each are explicit about who their ideal candidates are. Also, testimonials on the website and fellows featured as exemplary past recipients are not only a sound guide to the student's desirability as a candidate but are resonant with terms and phrases that are clues to self-presentation. Moreover, if the subject of your student's proposed research is a specific cause or group of people, it can make sense to define what's at stake for the student personally in the topic they would pursue. By addressing this issue they can present themselves as someone with personal experience or authoritative knowledge of their subject.

Even so, your student shouldn't confuse the criteria that qualify them to apply for a fellowship with the characteristics that rank them among the most appealing candidates in the applicant pool. They can be sure that if diversity is a key factor in selection, everyone else who is applying satisfies the fellowship's eligibility criteria, so belonging to a specific community or group is necessary but will not alone make them deserving of the opportunity they're seeking. What every one of these scholarships wants to know, essentially, is how they "add to the conversation" about diversity.[3] While fellowships increasingly seek candidates who embody a wide range of people who, typically, have not filled the ranks of university faculties, the judiciary, public service, or other highly sought-after positions, it is important for your students to be able to articulate precisely why diversity is meaningful to them or how their voice is representative of a previously silenced or overlooked point of view. Can they write about experiences that shed light on their relations with others and give them a window into the ways in which their situation or appearance affects how others perceive them? Do their beliefs, self-presentation, or identity give them experiences and special insight into social phenomena or cultural differences that are not widely understood or appreciated?

Whatever their experience, they should take care to think of themselves as someone in charge of their own destiny. If they've experienced a slight or even a serious injustice, for instance, how have they worked to rise above or move past it?

Consider, as well, the several ways their differences from others have enabled them to contribute to others' success as well as their own. In other words, even as they ponder the disadvantages they and others have faced—indeed, continue to confront—they should consider, as well, what they have gained and how they've been strengthened by the many ways being on the margins has prepared them to deal with unfamiliar and uncomfortable situations.

What follows is the introduction to the personal statement of a student who deciphers the enigma presented by who she *appears to be* on paper (the basis for what readers will assume about her) and what strangers experience when they first encounter her—not the person they imagined or anticipated. In fact, because she was named after a white American celebrity of the 1990s, the curiosity of the person reading her name, whether the *maître d'* at a restaurant or a member of an admissions committee, will be piqued: her *name* captures their attention.

> My parents named me "Demi Moore" to make me salient on paper—whether in resume piles or on restaurant reservation lists. They named me Demi Moore so that I would not have to fight the world as hard as it would fight me. On paper at least, I would be ageless and racially ambiguous. For years, I told a version of this story that cast my Black immigrant parents as longtime admirers of a popular American actress from the nineties, whom they chose as my namesake. I thought that the more complicated truth would get easier to tell with time. But both people and places deal in creation myths; this narrative thread has only gotten longer.
>
> My name represents one of many iterations of assimilation in the U.S., and more specifically, what my parents believed was worth passing down to me. The tension between my name and its implicit history has led me to strike a delicate balance between my privilege of looking at the "American Dream" through a fresh pair of eyes and the truth I share with those excluded from the promises of justice, fairness, and equality. Happy accidents like my own make for a rather uncertain foundation on which to structure life.[4]

Note the skill with which Demi unravels the complexity of her identity—what it means both literally and figuratively for her parents on a few levels. Literally, it acts as an attention-getter ("salient on paper"); metaphorically, it is a shield ("so that I would not have to fight the world as hard as it would fight me"), and a sheath ("ageless and racially ambiguous"). But then she further complicates "who she is" by discussing the tension between her name and "its implicit history"; that is, the promise of the American Dream "through a fresh pair of eyes" and those "excluded from the promises of justice." The only thing separating her, it seems, from "the excluded" is the accident of birth. Her parents are Black immigrants, but they are also solidly middle-class Americans.

Just as looks can deceive, so can words and names. Who she is, then, is a combination of image, perception, good fortune, and her family's history.

Perhaps Demi's example is so unusual, involving as it does someone explaining who she is by unpacking her relationship to a well-known celebrity who is a stranger to her, that your students may feel there is little they can learn from such a novel situation. In fact, however, any of us who ponder the circumstances of our upbringing are likely to be able to identify in ourselves features both recognizable and anomalous, which if explained, allow us to enable others to see the logic of who we are, what we care about, and what motivates us to act.

Even fellowships without a mandate to promote diversity often provide the option to supply a diversity statement. One of my advisees used the opportunity to think about how the many ways she differs from others have made her a better learner, a better scientist, and a more confident, developing scholar:

> As a child who learned English as a second language after immigrating, I recall not looking or sounding like most of my peers, who frequently reminded me of this throughout grade school. Learning to be comfortable with being different from those around me prepared me for many of my future experiences. For example, I have often been the youngest member of the research teams I have been on. This might be intimidating for most students but has allowed me to gain invaluable mentorship by experts in my field. Because I often find I have the most to learn, I am never ashamed to ask questions and gain new insight. This also prepared me for joining a social psychology lab where I was the only member whose background was not in psychology; there I've used my biology background to design studies that combine social and behavioral science. As a Muslim woman and first-generation college student, I'm often surrounded in academic and research settings by people whose backgrounds differ from my own. Yet having the courage to pursue these opportunities, despite feeling out of place, has given me the means to bring the scientific method to other realms. My background in contrasting fields allowed me to make the informed decision to pursue immunology research as a career and gave me the confidence to endure the challenges I will encounter in my professional journey. In the process, I have become captivated with the experience of defining unknowns through research.[5]

The power of this student's statement, even though she embodies an array of historically underrepresented students—a young woman majoring science, an immigrant whose first language is not English, one whose parents are working class, a member of the first generation in her family to attend college, and a Muslim—surprises her reader by describing how these attributes actually provided her with a range of experiences that allow her to be "comfortable with being uncomfortable," and thus a better learner: someone unafraid to ask questions, someone who seeks out mentoring, someone whose disciplinary training adds a different perspective to the project at hand. Each of these ultimately enabled her to cultivate self-confidence and a sense of mastery in her discipline. In other words, she conveys exquisitely how she "adds to the conversation" on diversity.

For fellowships *not* singularly designed to attract one kind of student or a commitment to a specific cause, however, it's important to understand that using language that ties your student to a set of social attributes without reflection or explanation may *narrow* rather than deepen the readers' comprehension of them as a candidate. In an essay that is a thousand words or less, your students may be tempted to describe themselves in the way they are accustomed to when they're among people with an intuitive grasp of what it means to inhabit overlapping identities. But the crux of the challenge all applicants face is to describe who they are, what they care about, and why to strangers whose only loyalty is to the process of selecting the most outstanding candidates. Application readers need to see "the person" come alive on the page: someone who will set their aspirations into motion by the force of their humanity, experience, and ambition. That's why to make themselves and their best ambitions understood it's necessary to convert language they commonly use among people whose ideals and opinions they share—an internal dialogue—into the language of the public square. So, again, your students need to show their readers who they are, not just "tell" what can only be appreciated by those who travel in the same circles.

Readers of fellowship applications care about the aims of the fellowship and strive to choose candidates whose purpose speaks to its mission and have the capacity to carry out the project they propose. But that is merely necessary, not sufficient. What makes a candidate rise above the necessary and the sufficient is a narrative that the reader not only explicitly but also *intuitively* connects to the ideals articulated by the fellowship's goals—a personal statement that creates the conditions in which the reader will readily "see" the applicant as exemplifying the purpose of the fellowship and the ideals of the organization that funds it. In other words, your students need to keep in mind not only what their readers understand to be the purpose of the fellowship they represent but *how* their readers will absorb what your students say about themselves.

Finally, your students should take care not to deprive their readers of the joy of discovery and recognition. As fellowship advisors, each of us has experienced the psychological pleasure of unearthing a diamond in the rough—the student others somehow overlooked; a young person whose blend of qualities, experiences, and skills uniquely qualifies them for a particular fellowship. Your job as a trusted reader is to know your applicants well enough not only to steer them away from oversharing but to coax from them details of their life stories that enable other readers to comprehend the beauty and potential you see in them. An essay that evokes a reader's sense of that young person's possibility is precisely why the personal statement has such a powerful influence on the way they will be perceived by a committee of fellowship readers. It is often why one candidate is favored over others. It is the writer's ability to translate their experience and ambitions into a portrait of someone readers believe is destined to fulfill the mission of the fellowship that will determine that applicant's success. The following exercise is designed to help your students think about themes that run through their disparate activities, interests, and commitments and to reflect on how they may speak to their intellectual missions.

> **REFLECTION: CONNECT THE DOTS BETWEEN YOUR INTERESTS, COMMITMENTS, AND ACADEMIC OR VOCATIONAL EXPERIENCES**
>
> 1. Think about all of the ways you've chosen to spend your time (e.g., employment, internships, extracurriculars, recreation, community or public service). Write about which activities you chose to give up so that you had time to do another or keep another commitment, like a job. Do you regret any of these decisions? Why or why not?
> 2. Do you see a relationship between any of these activities? Did performing one help you decide to or enable you to pursue another?
> 3. Write about the similarities between or among any of the activities you performed over an extended period of time. Is there an overall theme you can discern among a few or several of these activities?
> 4. Write about your leadership experiences. Bear in mind that "leadership" includes many kinds of engagement, from being the official head of an organization to being a steady influence on the way a group sets its goals or implements them. Answer as many of the following questions as you can.[6]
>   a. Have you ever helped to bring about change? If so, describe how.
>   b. How have you contributed to a group's ability to work well together?
>   c. Describe a time when you've helped a group face and overcome a challenge.
>   d. Discuss a time when your absence from a group would have affected its ability to reach its goals.
>   e. Describe a situation in which you changed others' minds.
>   f. Have you started a student (or other) organization whose mission was to solve a particular problem or unmet need?

g. In what ways have you used your abilities to identify and understand problems and opportunities, design solutions and implement them, recruit others to join an effort, and reach a desired result?
h. Discuss an instance in which you assumed a role in an organization and influenced its direction or helped to make it more effective.

NOTES

1. Daniel Hickey, interview with the author, Hunter College, February 23, 2022.
2. Alice Tsai, draft of personal statement for medical school application, spring 2021.
3. I am deeply indebted to Karilyn Crockett, Assistant Professor of Urban History, Public Policy & Planning at MIT, for her critique of this chapter and her guidance on this topic.
4. Demi Moore, personal statement, law school and fellowship applications, 2020.
5. Maisha Uddin, draft of Goldwater Scholarship diversity statement, January 2022.
6. The questions posed in item four were drawn from the Schwarzman Scholarship application.

Chapter 5

Framing the Narrative: Authenticity in the Personal Statement

By the time your students begin drafting their personal statements, there isn't much they can do to change the other parts of their applications: their transcripts, their academic achievements and awards to date, their extracurricular activities, internships, jobs, skills, and other interests, and what their recommenders will say about them in their letters of reference are all, at that point, beyond their ability to influence. Perhaps even more worrying (for them), on paper they will appear astonishingly similar to other candidates. A personal statement that *sings* can't overcome the most exceptional achievements of other candidates. But if your student's qualifications are even roughly comparable to those of past winners, they may be serious contenders. The personal statement then becomes the most significant influence on their chances of winning the fellowships they're applying for.

The best personal statements are born of introspection and the drudgery of drafting and repeated revision. In this chapter, we'll explore the primary issues any student needs to consider to make their finest effort, and we'll walk through the process of writing the personal statement. The key to the best personal statement is *authenticity* because this is what will set a student's application apart from other candidates. But beware, authenticity is not easy to locate. Your student's most-trusted mentors can point them in the right direction, but ultimately, only your student can identify what truly represents who they are. Only they really know themselves, the experiences that have shaped them, who they are, and what drives them.

The "intellectual mission" of the application—what your student hopes to pursue if they win a fellowship—is paramount and the key feature of the fellowship application. If a student's intellectual mission lacks originality or promise, the application will fail, so make no mistake about its centrality. Still, the number of words "spent" on the intellectual mission will vary from application to application. For a National Science Foundation Graduate Research Fellowship, for instance, there is nothing your students can say about themselves that will transcend their perceived luminance as future scientists. For the Marshall, Luce, or Beinecke Scholarships, for example, the proportions are different. Social and personal context must frame the intellectual mission persuasively or they will be one among many applicants whose candidacy will falter. The successful candidate will be the one whose path to and through college persuasively informs their intellectual mission. Regardless of whether the ratio of the intellectual mission to the "personal" part of their personal essays is small or large, its power to influence their readers is acute.

STRUCTURING THE ESSAY

Most advice will tell fellowship application writers to begin with a "hook" to capture the readers' interest partway in to the first paragraph. Such a device can be helpful but also misleading. An arresting anecdote, though captivating, must be thoroughly integrated into the candidate's purpose, personally, intellectually, and professionally. As they begin drafting their essay, it's good to remember that there's no such thing as a perfect personal statement and no formula for writing one. I worked with a student several years ago named Hassaan Shahawy, who was offered both the Rhodes and the Marshall Scholarships. Hassaan's early drafts for his Marshall application began with a vignette to draw his reader into the essay.[1] He brought in past experiences that illustrated the opening theme and transitioned to his "future plans and dreams." He ended with a rationale for applying for the fellowship and how it related to what he wanted to accomplish and "echoed" the introduction in his concluding paragraph. He worked on his essay for weeks, fiddling with sentences and word choice. As September approached, he had what he thought was a penultimate draft and showed his essay to his older sister. Her general impression was favorable, but she told him that it wasn't clear to her *why* he wanted to go to graduate school. She then made what turned out to be a definitive suggestion: "move up toward the top of the essay the reason you need this fellowship." His *motive*, the idea that had animated his choice of extracurriculars, his spiritual life, and what he hoped to study in the UK had been buried two-thirds of the way down his essay. Instead, she suggested, he should use it to create a frame through which his readers could view his candidacy.

Hassaan's impression that successful essays tend to conform to a predictable structure was well-founded. Like many schools, his university maintains an archive thick with winning essays from the most prestigious international scholarships its alumni have applied for over the years for future candidates to learn from, and Hassaan is a discerning student of prose. But the most effective personal essays are anything but formulaic. *Formula* partakes of structure, and while effective writing always has a structure (components and shape), formula and structure are not the same thing. Below we will discuss the parts of the personal statement, keeping in mind that the point of imposing a structure on an

FRAMING THE NARRATIVE

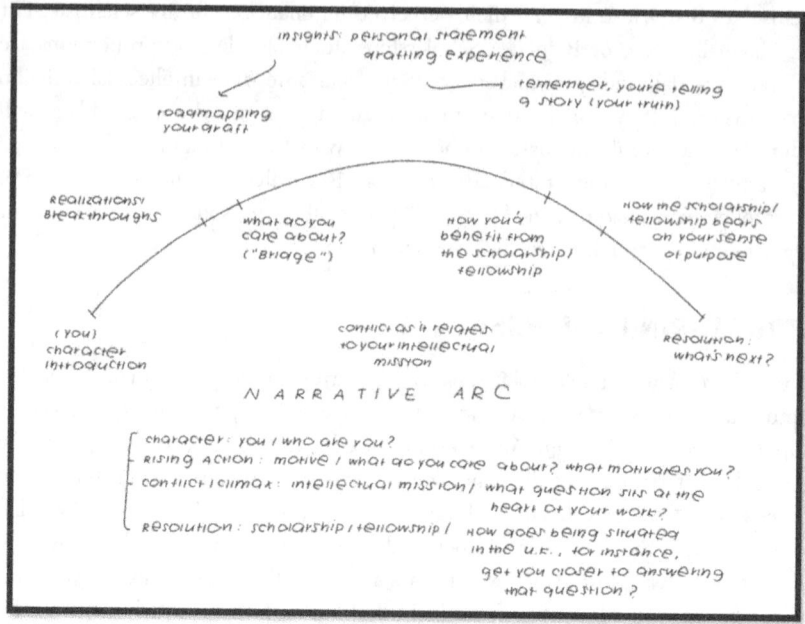

Figure 5.1 Narrative Arc. Illustration by Demi Moore, 2023

essay is to create a device that the reader can use to quickly grasp the significance of what the writer wants to achieve and why they want to achieve it.[2]

Above all, your candidates have to understand that *they're telling a story*. Stories make us alive and memorable to others, especially to people who don't know us. Like the classic narrative arc in storytelling (see Figure 5.1), the personal statement has four essential elements: character, tension, climax, resolution.[3] For the purposes of writing the personal statement it's easiest to think of these fundamental elements as answers to four questions: (1) Who are you? (2) What motivates you? (3) What is your intellectual mission? and (4) Why do you need this fellowship?

"Who you are" is the "personal" part of the personal statement; what makes a student's experience, interests, and skills distinct. What motivates them forms a "bridge" to the intellectual mission: the bridge explains why and how they became interested in the topic that has become their intellectual mission. Their intellectual mission forms the core of their self-narrative. It marks them as someone who has something important to contribute to their field of study—someone who will make an impact as an intellectual or a leader in the future. "Why you need this" summarizes what makes a student an appealing applicant and can provide the fellowship committee with a persuasive rationale for choosing your student over other candidates.

The content of the bridge, as we will see, can vary from one essay to another. An anecdote about a formative experience may form the bridge for the intellectual journey in one version of an applicant's personal statement, while for another fellowship application, the bridge could concern a moment of intellectual insight. Either approach may elucidate the motives for the student's intellectual mission, but one may be more appropriate or compelling in one context than the other. In composing a bridge, a student confronts the paradox of the personal statement: they need to present themselves as someone whose aims and ideals speak to the mission of the fellowship they're applying for. Their impulse may be to portray the person they believe the fellowship committee will think most deserves its support. Yet, what many applicants fail to understand as they sit down to compose their personal statements is that what makes them most appealing as candidates is simply who they are. As we've discussed earlier, however ordinary your students may seem to themselves, their personal qualities and experiences are the very characteristics that will make them stand out among other candidates. This is why a faithful presentation of self—authenticity—is the most important feature of a successful personal statement; a form of creative nonfiction that distills what is most distinctive about your student. An applicant should approach the personal statement with imagination and describe their mission with the care of someone narrating a culminating, potentially life-changing experience.

Authenticity dwells in the relationship between who a student is, what they care about, and why. In the authentic personal statement, a student's interests reveal an internal consistency and, ideally, form a motif. The reader's sense that the applicant's innate qualities, learning, and experiences have combined to propel them toward an intellectual mission expresses something essential about them and becomes the glue that binds together all the parts of the application. Another seeming contradiction: a student might think that an authentic representation of who they are could only ever tell the same story. After all, if the story they tell expresses something genuine about themselves and is internally consistent, it might seem there would only be a single way of telling it. Yet, each time a student writes a personal statement they could tell a different story from a different perspective. In one perhaps your student is a daughter or son; in another they're someone who has been profoundly affected by a mentor or a friend or even a stranger; in yet another they are someone who has left their small town, deserted their faith or returned to it, served in the military, started a community service organization, or learned a life-lesson. But understand this, which ever "version" of themselves they present, if it speaks to the values and goals that matter to them most, they are representing themselves authentically.

The issues that matter to your students most are usually those they've learned to speak about as a kind of "passion."[4] And again, as I've already pointed out, they've probably been encouraged at some point by a well-meaning adult—usually someone highly accomplished and secure in their success, to "follow your bliss." Similarly, most fellowship applicants are urged to name what they are passionate about in their personal statements, and some fellowship essay prompts even ask applicants explicitly to discuss their "passion." But I suggest students avoid the word itself if they can. Yes, they need to convey that they care deeply, *fervently*, about what matters to them but they should care enough, too, not to use the same language as every other applicant to describe what motivates them.[5]

So, for example, the first thought that routinely occurs to a student beginning to write a personal statement for a medical school application is some variation on the idea that they want to become a doctor "to help people." This is a noble and, one hopes, a necessary sentiment for a future physician. Indeed, we all want to be effective at whatever we do for a living—"to make a difference"—so it takes little imagination to understand how gratifying it must feel to be a person whose livelihood relieves others' suffering or lengthens lives. Many of the essays written by medical school applicants also poignantly invoke a family member who suffered from a life-threatening illness that caused the author to resolve, at a young age, to prevent others from enduring the same fate.

Understandably, then, the aspiring medical student is "passionate" about becoming a doctor. But they need to think, additionally, about what *specific* difference their becoming a doctor could make. What would they add to the world of people dedicated to caring for those with the most chronic or horrific diseases? The same applies to the would-be philosopher, mathematician, artist, or political scientist. What difference, for instance, would a student's contribution make to the way political scientists think about sustaining healthy democracies worldwide? Or (a more intimate personal example, perhaps) how would a student's experience as the eldest child of a single parent inform the way they think about the needs of families under stress during the Covid-19 pandemic, or food insecurity, or an under-resourced school straining to deal with the technological challenges of remote learning? Applicants will find that they do a much better job articulating what animates them and why if they avoid the word passion in describing it. Instead, they should focus on *purpose*.[6] By explaining their purpose, they reveal their passions. Their readers will then have a better, more organic understanding of why they care rather than *that* they care, simply because they emphatically say they do.

The act of describing the difference they hope to make will show their readers their enthusiasm for solving the important problems in their discipline—whether it is painting, politics, or physics. Ultimately, representing themselves authentically in a personal essay not only makes a student a more appealing candidate; it gets them closer to what they care about. Once they have clarified this, they will be able to fuse their true selves with work that matters to them and others over the length of their working lives.

LEADING THE READER ACROSS "THE BRIDGE": MOTIVE, AIM, AND ACTION

The bridge in the personal essay is where motive is expressed and makes clear for the reader *why* the applicant is doing, or wants to do, what they profess. Often an effective bridge can be found in the student's biography. Contemplation of the trials or ordinary pleasures of one's past can be newly understood as a source of wonder about the world at large. Perhaps the student learned something that changed the way they view people with cognitive disabilities, realized an injustice they had been impervious to previously, or saw beauty in how mRNA can be programmed to treat and prevent disease. A switch flipped and they realized what they wanted to do or who they wanted to be. Once they truly understand what motivates them, their goals and actions no longer exist in separation but link to a larger purpose.

An essay's bridge might describe an innovation a student pioneered that decisively affected the progress of everyone around them. I'm reminded of a student who designed a shortcut in her lab's research procedures that significantly reduced the time to complete necessary but lengthy experiments to bring about more rapid results. As a varsity swimmer, she was accustomed to working toward "personal bests" to chart her accomplishments. But this breakthrough benefitted everyone working in her lab and reinforced a major theme of her application, which extolled the excitement of teamwork in scientific research. Another student explained how, while taking a course on human trafficking, he first came to decipher the meaning of the "Missing" posters tacked to telephone poles all over his neighborhood when he was growing up. His bridge began with this slowly dawning realization and moved to other personal recollections as he summoned up the periodic, alarming, and unexplained disappearance of classmates from his community during his middle- and high-school years. As he makes this connection, first for himself, then as reconstructed for his reader, his stake in the social problem he hopes to untangle with the help of a fellowship comes forcefully into view. But it serves the same function as the bridge that begins with an autobiographical detail. It doesn't replace the necessary biographical and "personal" part of the personal statement; it simply supplies a different starting point. Still, whether your student begins their essay with a reflection on a formative moment in their upbringing or a flash of insight, the bridge creates a place in their essay to talk about motive, purpose, and critically, their intellectual mission, the centerpiece of the personal statement. It links the "who" at one end with the "how" at the other, by providing the reader with a sensible, earnest construction of the "why" in between, which brings the fellowship committee to the student's reason for wanting the fellowship.

INTELLECTUAL MISSION

Unlike the personal statement for a college admissions application, the heart of the personal statement for a fellowship is the intellectual puzzle your student hopes to solve—their intellectual mission. The intellectual mission must be readily perceived as valid and important: readers of the application want to know whether the candidate's interests will matter either to an academic discipline, to the world at large, or both. They are also looking for people who will make change possible, for intellectual or political leaders, or scholars who will advance thinking in their chosen field.

Your student's description of their intellectual mission may be a story of development and discovery. As when they applied to college, they remain open to new discoveries. What is more, they are now able to exploit such discoveries in ways they weren't back when they applied to college because they now have the tools to do so. But explaining their intellectual mission is essential. For many applicants the impetus for action will be an event that stands next to or even outside the puzzle they're trying to solve. It supplies a motive for undertaking the intellectual mission that acts like a motor attached to a boat, propelling it forward.

Is it less effective for a student to pose an intellectual puzzle or scientific problem as the thing that inspires them, detached from personal involvement? Not at all. Their motive for being interested in a problem in philosophy, classics, or economics could arise entirely from the intellectual pleasure they derive from attempting to solve it. Even so, it may also contain an aspect of individual or personal connection that makes the problem particularly intriguing for them. If they can unpack the fascination they experience, describe the aesthetic elegance of a conundrum in their field, or convey the neglected importance of answering the question that is their intellectual mission, they will have ended in the same place. But minimally, they need to explain its significance in comprehensible, palpable, arresting terms. In other words, they have to answer the "So what?" question: why does it matter, to whom does it matter, and what is its relative importance to the problems people in their field are trying to solve? More than any other aspect of their fellowship application, the intellectual mission most resembles the essays they will write for admission to graduate school. There they will be asked to identify general areas of inquiry and the questions they hope to pose and answer. The difference, however, is that, whereas for their graduate school application they can assume that their reader understands the rhetoric of their specific discipline and expects them to employ it as a way of demonstrating their sophistication and knowledge of the field, for most fellowship applications that isn't the case. Your student shouldn't assume that their readers are familiar with their discipline's vocabulary; they have to approach their essays, above all, as acts of translation.

The applicant's job is to find the balance between describing the frontiers of their field in comprehensible terms and why they should matter to someone who is intelligent, experienced, and well-read but knows little about that field.[7] Let's consider an example, one I introduced earlier in this chapter, when describing the challenges of giving the personal statement the proper "shape" and organization. As we'll see, Hassaan Shahawy employs a light touch in connecting his interest in Islam's place in the modern world with the legacy of colonialism. Rather than delving into postcolonial theory or a specific critique of the domination of Muslim societies by colonial powers in the modern era, he simply recognizes its "disastrous effects," and moves on. Shahawy's personal statement is, in many ways, a model of its kind, so we will spend the remainder of this chapter parsing its narrative arc to discuss each component and why it works.

SAMPLE ESSAY: "WHERE ARE YOU GOING?"

Shahawy's personal statement is satisfying on its face: eloquently written, it projects the author's sense of purpose, a clear intellectual mission, and a sound rationale for why he wants the scholarship. But it also displays perceptible stylistic integrity—vivid description, pleasing structure, and rhetorical resonance. These features are all immediately apparent, so even if one reads the essay hastily without lingering on its details, it feels "complete." Yet if you look carefully at its constituent parts, you'll see that there is a great deal more to appreciate about it. Below I've identified the essay's four distinct parts, which represent the essential elements of any personal statement. Following that, I've reproduced Shahawy's text, and beneath each section of text, I analyze how it works and what he accomplishes in it.

The "classic" narrative arc of Shahawy's essay:

1. *Character* ("who"): An anecdote, which introduces the character(s); an (inner) conflict, which yields to the applicant's motive for past and future actions, and points to an intellectual mission.
2. *Rising action* ("the character's journey"): A rationale for commitments, i.e., their motivation or "bridge," but also a conventional narration of accomplishments that offers a coherent picture of the applicant's behavior and choices.
3. *Conflict/climax* ("intellectual mission"): An explanation of the applicant's intellectual mission (e.g., "why Oxford," and why law school afterwards).
4. *Resolution* ("why they need this fellowship"): A transcendent understanding of self and one's purpose in life.

Part one:

"Where are you going?" (Qur'an 81:26). I first interpreted this verse to mean one thing: I needed to be going somewhere. To me, it meant to walk with purpose, a message that resonated with the way I was raised. That changed when, as a freshman in college, I joined a prison mentorship program and visited a prison for the first time. Just minutes into meeting my assigned inmate, I realized he was a remarkable man. Growing up, negative influences had pressured him into crime. In prison, however, his regret had fueled a powerful transformation. Despite this, he would not be eligible for parole for twenty years. I felt conflicted, as perhaps there are crimes for which regret cannot atone, but I knew that this man's mistakes were the result of more than his own choices. As the visit continued, I realized that I could not mentor such a man, for through his sincerity and passion for learning, he was the one teaching me. Suddenly, a bell rang, bringing him to his feet. "Where are you going?" I asked. Smiling, he answered, "Back to my cell."

"Where are you going?" I had asked, forgetting that he only had one place to go. To my right a man kissed his wife goodbye, and to my left a little girl begged her daddy to come home. It was bewildering, seeing captivity and freedom embrace before the free walked out an open door and the jailed back into their cells. I left the prison, but all around, I felt the prisons of social injustices marginalizing their inmates. I remembered the prisons of my family history, the political prisons of 1950s Egypt, where the regime tortured my grandfather for his activism. I reflected on my prison of being a Muslim-American during the War on Terror, in which I fight to remind others that I, too, am America. I saw then that society was filled with prisons, all marginalizing their inmates and leaving many with nowhere to go. Whether it was the convict caught in the cycle of recidivism or the Muslim alienated by Islamophobia, I became committed to addressing the systemic injustices that rob the underprivileged of opportunity.

The essay begins with a phrase from the Qur'an, which serves a dual purpose: it hints at the writer's identity as a Muslim and poses a question that all fellowship applications implicitly ask: "who are you and *where are you going?*" Shahawy also speaks of "purpose," which he interprets at this point in his evolution as understanding that he needs to be going, or walking somewhere, "with purpose." He volunteers to mentor a prison inmate, a hopeful gesture, a down payment on his purpose. Or so it seems.

Analyzing this essay in a writing workshop one year elicited an unexpected, astonishing response from one of our students—one that hadn't occurred before. He observed that Shahawy, in choosing to write about mentoring an inmate, seemed to be making a conspicuous display of his virtue. I asked the workshop's other students whether the author's seeming "altruism" struck them, too, as calculated or insincere. They were mixed in their interpretations of his motives. They did agree, however, that sincere or not, by citing an example of "good works," Shahawy had engaged in a familiar convention of personal statement writing, which is to highlight one's acts of selflessness. This, some of them pointed out, was followed by yet another convention of the genre, when Shahawy insists that the inmate, the object of his good works, had more to teach him than he himself had to offer in return.

Suddenly, however, Shahawy turns convention on its head by disclosing his evident embarrassment at what transpires next: As their meeting ends, Shahawy asks the inmate, reflexively, "Where are you going?" When the prisoner responds to the writer's question, "smiling," Shahawy realizes immediately how thoughtless he has been by posing this question to someone he *knows* has nowhere else to go—someone whose imprisonment, in fact, is the author's very reason for being there. Subtly he illuminates the gentle wisdom of his incarcerated "host," whose reply winks at the author's apparent obliviousness. The rhetorical echoing of the passage from the Qur'an—Shahawy's noting that he asked his host, "Where are you going?"—reveals his shallowness to himself, the juxtaposition of perfunctory small talk (the essence of the profane) with the sacred text he quotes at the outset. The distance between word and deed. The refrain, moreover, has the effect of creating a motif in the essay, for he repeats the phrase three times. His description of his surprising encounter with the inmate suggests, further, that Shahawy's earlier use of such time-worn features of the personal statement was strategic: by playing on the sort of modulated virtue-signaling one expects in a personal statement, he amplifies the reader's reaction to his gaffe, which is deployed like the walloping punchline of a joke.

This pivotal second paragraph provides the bridge for Shahawy's essay. By offering an occasion for the writer to consider who is free and who is not free and why, the passage triggers a spiritual and intellectual transfiguration as he connects his realization to an academic mission and purpose in life. This gives way to a revealing discussion of the author's own family history with detention, torture, and injustice—reasons they left their homeland for the United States—and injustices that might threaten his family again in their adopted land, and in fact all Muslim-Americans too, because of rising anti-Muslim sentiment. The second paragraph functions as the essay's bridge because it supplies the motive for what Shahawy wants to do with his life and why. Thus, he reasons, during his time in the United Kingdom, he wants to study how systemic injustice robs the underprivileged of opportunity.

Part two:

> Through my work with marginalized communities, I came to believe in the importance of community institutions in combatting these systemic injustices. I learned this firsthand in my work with the American Civil Liberties Union (ACLU), where I monitored the treatment of inmates with disabilities in Los Angeles County jails. Through the ACLU, I also participated in workshops hosted by Homeboy Industries, a startup that employs former convicts in its businesses around Los Angeles. By operating as a business, Homeboy provides former inmates with economic security while ensuring the sustainability of its social services. Inspired by Homeboy's effectiveness, I sought work experience at international startups like Liwwa Inc. to learn how to leverage for-profit mechanisms for global social impact.

> At the same time, my work with Muslim institutions, such as directing national camps for the Muslim Youth of North America, showed me how healthy mosques and community spaces can transform the lives of Muslim-Americans. In these centers, Muslims feeling alienated from society can learn from scholars who study Islam's relationship to the modern. This field is one of my own academic passions, specifically the mechanisms by which Islamic law demands adjustment to social change and modernization. By bringing this jurisprudence to Muslims through community institutions, I aim to help Muslims navigate the tensions between their religious identities and their lives in secular societies. In challenging the assumption that the two are incompatible, I also work to undermine the extremist ideologies that use tensions between Islam and the West to fuel violence, showing how their claims are antithetical to Islam's legal methodology.

These two paragraphs review the writer's commitment to working locally to advance the cause of marginalized people, from inmates with disabilities to current and former prisoners to Muslim youths. This portion of the essay comes closest to the kind of "brag sheet" so many candidates produce to provide a guided tour through their résumés. However, it transcends this objective by describing the author's interest in helping Muslim-American youths adapt the religious laws of their people to contemporary American culture, which poses secular challenges to their faith and the sustenance of community. While many see the two cultures as incompatible, Shahawy says he believes that tensions between the two cultures can be productively mediated through Muslim community institutions.

Part three:

> To pursue this goal, I need a program that synthesizes classical Islamic studies with modern Islamic thought—a trait unique to Oxford's MPhil in Islamic Studies and History. In the program, I would study Islamic history with renowned classicists like Professor Christopher Melchert, while examining Islam's place in modernity with Professor Tariq Ramadan, an authority in the field. Yet given colonialism's disastrous effects on the Muslim world, there is dissonance in my hoping to be a Rhodes Scholar, a program founded upon a colonialist conception of elitist leadership. As a student whose identity and research work to bridge the demographic complexities of postcolonial civilization, I hope to address this colonial legacy head-on, pushing the cultures of Oxford to engage with non-Western epistemologies. I hope to do the same beyond Oxford by participating in British Muslim communities, which have been more successful than their American counterparts at gaining prominence in public discourse. As I learn from their achievements, I aim to forge partnerships between Muslim institutions of the two nations that would

strengthen both communities, helping them find their place in the national identities of their respective homelands.

After the program, I would hope to pursue a JD/PhD in comparative law, while also studying criminal law and policy. Equipped with these tools, I would be ready to build initiatives that offer marginalized communities the support they need. I hope to do this as a law professor, through which I would continue my research in comparative law, while working within my academic institution to develop community programs and legal clinics that help people on a daily basis. Eventually, I hope to apply this expertise to electoral politics, where I aim to be a voice for the marginalized in political discourse.

In this section Shahawy states his reason for wanting to study at Oxford (which is required by the scholarship's guidelines) and lays out his "intellectual mission" when he says, "As a student whose identity and research work to bridge the demographic complexities of postcolonial civilization, I hope to address this colonial legacy head-on, pushing the cultures of Oxford to engage with non-Western epistemologies." Here he provides a rationale both for why and where he wants to study and how it relates to his purpose: "to be a voice for the marginalized in political discourse." This section is closest to the content and thrust of a graduate school personal statement, as it creates a rationale for being at a specific institution (i.e., "why he needs this fellowship"), studying under the influence of notable faculty in his intended field of interest.

Part four:

"Where are you going?" At first, it motivated me to be going somewhere, then reminded me to be thankful to have somewhere to go. Yet in its original Arabic, the question is not asked with the singular "you," but with the plural. By definition, I cannot answer it alone. So as I go forward, constantly shaping the vision of my destination, the verse reminds me of my obligation to take others forward with me. I want to be a Rhodes Scholar to fulfill that obligation.

Shahawy begins his brief concluding paragraph with the by-now familiar, "Where are you going?" This kind of symmetrical mirroring of the opening paragraph can be an effective stylistic device, as it brings us full circle, back to where we began. What is more, in this case, because the phrase has been employed four times, it acts as an aesthetically pleasing literary maneuver, in the manner of a ritualistic refrain, like a scripted response to a prayer. But even more satisfying is that Shahawy makes clear that his understanding of "where he is going" is informed by his growing sophistication as a reader of Arabic and, by implication, of the Qur'an: his comprehension of the meaning of the phrase repurposes his belief that he, as an individual, needs to be going somewhere as someone who belongs with others, all going forward together toward their destination. His purpose has been transformed in response to his new view of himself, or his new view of "you," as he says, in the "plural." And note, he never uses the word "lead" or "leadership" in reference to himself, even though subliminally, the essay is about transforming himself into a leader who "takes others forward" with him. His altered understanding of the phrase that begins and ends the essay skillfully weaves together his "good works," his identity, his intellectual mission, a transformed understanding of what it means to lead, and his personal, spiritual, and professional ambitions.

Now let's return to what I referred to earlier as the essential elements of the narrative arc and think about how they apply to Shahawy's personal statement. To review, the elements are answers to four questions: (1) Who are you? (2) What motivates you? (3) What is your intellectual mission? and (4) Why do you need this fellowship? "Seeing captivity and freedom embrace" is the crucial phrase in Shahawy's essay. In a single scene he recreates the moment when an acute moral realization unfolded for him. It gathers together all the themes that thread their way through his personal, social, political, and intellectual concerns: his family's history, his faith, his concerns about alienating marginalized members of society, his interest in law, history, and concepts of justice—all of these live in the space between freedom and captivity.

Figure 5.2 Rhodes Scholar Hassaan Shahawy, University of Oxford, 2020. Photograph courtesy of Hassaan Shahawy

One of the greatest challenges I face in helping a student fuse aspects of their experience with the intellectual journey they hope to undertake in a fellowship is to help them plumb the sources of their inspiration. One way for your students to accomplish this for themselves is to review their answers to the "Inventory of Purpose" exercise at the end of Chapter 1, and the "Connecting the Dots" exercise at the end of Chapter 2. Identifying prominent themes can help them make sense of their curricular choices, the ways they spend time outside of the classroom, and the kind of "meaning making" that these commitments express. This understanding can, in turn, help them discern where they are headed intellectually and professionally and will form the basis for the narrative they construct in their personal statement. In the end, the "package" they present—their provenance and the person they have become, how they choose to spend their time, what they hope to accomplish in both the short and long term—should be someone that people close to them recognize. People who can affirm that the personal statement is a faithful rendering of the person they know—the student's authentic self.

*

The following exercise will help contextualize your student's intellectual mission, which will help them build a narrative that links their biography to their reason for wanting to carry out the work of the fellowship they're applying for.

EXERCISE: ACADEMIC INTERESTS AND ACHIEVEMENTS

1. What was your major in college and why did you choose it?
2. Which of the courses you've taken are thematically related to your proposed fellowship program? List up to five course titles with brief descriptions.
3. What was your most meaningful scholarly effort before you began your thesis or capstone?
4. How did you choose your thesis topic, why is it important to you, and what is its broader impact? How has it affected your intellectual, political, or social development? Which of your academic experiences have prepared you best for your plans after graduation (or for further study)?
5. Do you have any academic or intellectual role models? If so, who are they?
6. What are your academic interests outside your major? How have you pursued these interests through your coursework or extracurriculars?

7. Are you proficient or fluent in any languages other than English?
8. If you have studied, lived, worked, or had any experiences abroad, list when, where you were, and why you went there. How did this experience influence your studies, personal development, perspective, and shape postgraduate and career plans? Will you study or work abroad in the future? If so, when, where, and why?
9. Discuss why you've chosen your course of postgraduate study or intended career. What did you learn through your formal studies, extracurricular, and non academic experiences? Discuss an experience that informed or inspired your proposed project or fellowship.
10. Describe in no more than a paragraph your "intellectual mission" during the fellowship you hope to undertake.

NOTES

1. I want to thank Hassaan Shahawy (Harvard College, class of 2016; Rhodes Scholar, 2016) for sharing with me his insights into his essay-writing process. I also want to thank him for allowing me to teach his essay to my writing workshops twice each year.
2. Hassaan's essay is worth spending some time on to understand why it works so well as a personal statement. The full text is reproduced and examined later in this chapter, with his permission.
3. Thanks to Demi Moore for creating this illustration.
4. See, e.g., Steve Annear, "Bridgewater Student's Harvard Admissions Essay about Finding Passion for Life after Losing Her Mother to Cancer Goes Viral on TikTok: Yes, Abigail Mack Got In. She Begins Classes in the Fall," *Boston Globe*, updated May 12, 2021, www.bostonglobe.com/2021/05/12/metro/bridgewater-students-harvard-admissions-essay-about-finding-passion-life-after-losing-her-mother-cancer-goes-viral-tiktok/.
5. According to Google's "Books Ngram Viewer," which tracks historical trends in word usage in published books, between 1978 and 2019 the use of the word "passion" in printed sources increased by 217%. You may be surprised to learn, however, that the height of the use of "passion" in printed sources was in 1807. Between 1807 and 1978 (its nadir) its use declined by 87%, before being revived. See the Ngram Viewer, https://books.google.com/ngrams/graph?content=passion&year_start=1800&year_end=2019&corpus=en-2019&smoothing=3 at https://books.google.com/ngrams.
6. See William Damon, *The Path to Purpose: How Young People Find Their Calling in Life* (New York: Free Press, 2009), 33–34.
7. At the end of this chapter is an exercise to help a student begin to formulate an intellectual mission, if they have not already done so.

WORKS CITED

Annear, Steve. "Bridgewater Student's Harvard Admissions Essay about Finding Passion for Life after Losing Her Mother to Cancer Goes Viral on TikTok: Yes, Abigail Mack Got In. She Begins Classes in the Fall." *Boston Globe*, updated May 12, 2021. www.bostonglobe.com/2021/05/12/metro/bridgewater-students-harvard-admissions-essay-about-finding-passion-life-after-losing-her-mother-cancer-goes-viral-tiktok/.

Damon, William. *The Path to Purpose: How Young People Find Their Calling in Life*. New York: Free Press, 2009.

Google Books Ngram Viewer. "Passion." https://books.google.com/ngrams/graph?content=passion&year_start=1800&year_end=2019&corpus=en-2019&smoothing=3.

Chapter 6

Where to Begin? Getting Your Students Started on Writing Their Personal Statements

As a fellowship advisor, you know that there are as many good answers to the question "Where to begin?" as there are well-written personal statements and no one answer that's right for all writers.[1] To arrive at the answer that is right for your students, it is important for them to know themselves as writers. They may need to experiment a bit to find out what works best for them, or vary their approach, depending on what they're writing. If they are steadied by drafting an outline before they begin to write an essay, then they should outline. If outlines don't help them, they should just start writing. I know writers who outline as they write—mapping out, for example, each section of an essay just before they write it—and writers who outline what they've already written, to get some perspective on the structure of what they've written. These approaches work for them; they may or may not work for your students. But as Harry Bauld, who wrote *the* book on the college application essay thirty-five years ago, observes, "The hardest thing to do is to budge an object from a dead start, particularly if that object is your brain."[2]

Left to their own devices, many applicants will begin simply by "narrating" their résumés. "*I did this, which led to that, which gave me the experience to qualify for the other.*" The expediency of this approach is that it instantly creates the spine of a personal statement. It is also a dull and inescapable trap: once the student hangs their story on a sequence of personal successes, it can be really difficult for them to breathe life back into the narrative. Nonetheless, the best way for a student to begin is simply *to begin*, taking any approach that gets them going. In a chapter of his book called "Warming Up," Bauld offers the would-be essayist this advice: before you start working on a formal piece of writing, *practice* writing informally by "rambling" … for 250 words, or ten minutes, or by "free associating," "ranting," "grousing," or "writing fast" about something that bores you.[3] It's a start.

DOI: 10.4324/9781003455387-6

WHERE TO BEGIN?

Figure 6.1 Amanda Benoit Taveras and Maya Mouldi, Hunter College, 2023. Photograph by the author

In what follows, I offer additional suggestions for how to start—some that my colleague Margaret Sabin and I have used in a course we teach on the personal statement, including some that we have gathered from renowned writers and writing teachers, such as John McPhee, whose essays on writing are collected in his book *Draft No. 4*, and Marie Ponsot and Rosemary Deen, coauthors of a book on teaching writing titled *Beat Not the Poor Desk*.[4] Along the way I offer some writing exercises that we have adapted from our own experiences teaching writing in various contexts. I also add a little to what I've said in Chapter 5 about how to structure the final draft of the personal statement.

The suggestions I discuss for "how to begin" are:

- Freewrite
- Write a letter ("Dear Mother")
- Write the easiest part first ("Who am I?")
- Try one of five inspirational formulas
- Identify the bridge

*

FREEWRITE

In starting any piece of writing, John McPhee says, for him, "the hardest part comes first, getting something—anything—out in front of me. Sometimes in a nervous frenzy I just fling words as if I were flinging mud at a wall." His experience forms the basis for this suggestion for how to get started: "Blurt out, heave out, babble out something—anything—as a first draft. With that, you have achieved a sort of nucleus."[5] McPhee's comment on producing a first draft probably sounds a lot like advice your students' English teachers once gave them about producing an unseemly sounding "vomit draft": *Write down everything that occurs to you on a subject without self-censoring*. McPhee, as self-deprecating a writing teacher as there ever was, understands the fear of the uncomely first draft. Alluding to the horror story by Edgar Allan Poe, he refers to writing that draft as "the pit and the pendulum" phase of writing. He reminds the writer that whenever fear threatens to stop them in their tracks, it's essential to simply keep moving forward. He asks, "How could anyone ever know that something is good before it exists?" His point: until and unless you have a first draft, you can't know what in it works, what needs revising. And "unless you can identify what is not succeeding ... how are you going to be able to tone it up and make it work?"[6]

WRITE A LETTER ("DEAR MOTHER")

One of McPhee's most ingenious ploys for getting started on a piece of writing—a sort of trick to remove any mental and emotional roadblocks that may prevent the writer from beginning—is to suggest that the writer pretend that they are writing a letter to someone they are close to. In fact, he suggests, he gave this very advice to a former student (later a professional writer) who was "blocked," when writing an essay about a bear. He counseled the student to start off, "Dear Mother," and then proceed simply by describing his subject in the most literal fashion possible: "the bear has a fifty-five-inch waist and a neck more than thirty inches around but could run nose-to-nose with Secretariat."[7] The essence of the "Dear Mother" tactic for McPhee seems to be to apply the most literal approach possible in describing his subject, sweeping analysis and interpretation off the table. It keeps overthinking at bay. It enables the writer to create momentum, to get the ball rolling. If your students employ the "Dear Mother" tactic, they'll find it demystifies the process of writing, alleviates any worries they may have about "voice," "authority," or "audience," and allows them to express freely and without self-consciousness something they want to relate or describe. It gets them underway.[8]

WRITE THE EASIEST PART FIRST ("WHO AM I?")

Since personal statements are generally no more than 1,000 words, your students don't need to worry about not having enough to say—quite the contrary. One way to get started is for them to begin by drafting the section they know the most about, which is likely to be the one that concerns their intellectual mission. But a caution: a student may find that beginning with their intellectual mission bogs them down in the complexities of their specialty and prevents them from just "telling the thing as it is," which is what McPhee advises the writer to do when he suggests they begin by writing to their mother. Just as your student embarks on drafting a personal statement, they may become so caught up in describing their area of academic inquiry that they find it hard to write about the personal qualities or experiences that make them distinctive as a fellowship applicant and that motivated their inquiry in the first place. Therefore, your student may want to start by writing about who they are, which lends itself to a seamless transition to what matters to them and why. Chapter 3 discusses all the influences that contribute to who your student is at the moment they sit down to write their personal statement. The exercise, "When did you become *you*?" in Chapter 3 will be of great help to them as they sketch out the person behind the application.

TRY ONE OF FIVE INSPIRATIONAL FORMULAS

McPhee observes that in any narrative there is a contest between chronology and theme. "The narrative," he says, "wants to move from point to point through time, while topics that have arisen now and again across someone's life cry out to be collected. They want to draw themselves together in a single body, in the way that salt does underground. But chronology usually dominates."[9] In Chapter 5, I've described one way a student might structure an effective personal statement, by writing about the following topics in this order: (1) who they are; (2) what their motive is; (3) what they want to achieve (the intellectual mission); (4) why they need a particular fellowship to achieve it and what they will contribute to the mission of the foundation offering the fellowship. As we saw in the last example, these "essential elements" can be creatively rearranged to good effect. The order of what I have called (1) and (2) can be reversed but element (3) will supply the rationale for the fellowship, and (4) reminds the reader, "why *me*?" If a student chooses to structure a personal statement like this, the tension between chronology and theme will largely be resolved; the reader won't be confused about the relationship of time to theme when they link the personal to the intellectual through the structure proposed. However, the structure of the final draft does not have to dictate how the student begins.

Another idea for how to begin comes from Ponsot and Deen's *Beat Not the Poor Desk*.[10] They propose several ways of structuring essays, which they call "essay shapes," each composed in two parts, implicitly posing a question and a "reply." They describe each in a short-hand form with a brief formula. While their goal is to provide the writer with different ways to organize an essay, we offer their examples here as inspiration for how to begin writing a personal statement. Four of the five formulas noted below come from Ponsot and Deen; we have added a fifth:[11]

- Once _____. Now _____. (Where "now" simply means, "at a later moment.")
- They say _____. My research or analysis or experience shows _____.

WHERE TO BEGIN?

- On the one hand, _____. On the other hand, _____.
- That is the way it was, and it made this difference.
- In this dilemma or crisis, I turned to the following principle.

The idea is *not* literally and mechanically to employ one of the formulas in their own writing but rather to make some innovative use of the *concept* that it expresses, to get started.

How might these formulas inspire your students? They should ask themselves what they want to accomplish through their personal statements.

- Are they, for example, trying to show change over time? Then they will want to work with the concept of "once/now": they want to show how things were in (at least) two different moments in time—one earlier ("once") and one later ("now")—and explain what happened to bring about the change.
- Do they want to show how their research, analysis, or experience builds on and/or improves upon, or differs from, the work of others? Then they want to work with the concept of "they say": they want to show, first, what others did and then where their own work (their research, analysis, or experience) stands in relation to it.
- Does the answer to their question have two sides to it? They want to work with "on the one hand/on the other hand": they want to give each side its due.
- Are they trying to zero in on the critical cause, or causes, for a particular development, or sequence of developments? If they are, of course, they're trying to show change over time; they may be content to work with "once/now." But they may find more inspiration in the formula, "This is the way it was, and it made this difference," since it suggests a slightly different organization and emphasis: it suggests that their essay will begin by conjuring up one particular set of circumstances ("this is the way it was") and then explore what emerged as a result ("it made this difference").
- Do they want to focus on what motivated them to make a particular choice, or choices? "In this dilemma or crisis, I turned to the following principle" suggests one particular approach: first they describe the dilemma or crisis (or other type of situation); then they explain what they did and why. And while the formula speaks of "principle," they might choose to write about some completely different type of motivation.

Bear in mind that any one of these formulas can also be used to organize the final draft of the personal statement. Your students should also pay attention to the ways that the writers they particularly enjoy tend to organize their writing; these may reveal all kinds of ideas for their essay.

A good example of a final draft that employs the concept of "Once/Now" is Hassaan Shawhawy's essay that we examined in Chapter 5. He begins with one understanding of the phrase "Where are you going?" and emerges at the end with a fuller, more nuanced grasp of its meaning, of himself, and his purpose in life.[12] In an example from the Fulbright application of a student named Peter Leo, who is confronted by a difficult teaching challenge, he turns to the last of the organizing principles discussed above, "In this dilemma or crisis, I turned to the following principle":

> How do you take something you have known for your entire life, and teach it in a way that's totally different? This was the predicament I found myself faced with, late on a weeknight, stumped trying to plan my lesson. [W]orking at the FMDG music school for visually impaired students ... I had been tasked with introducing the trombone to five or six elementary school students, none of whom could see the instrument. As a trombonist of 13 years, I grew up with the trombone ... [but this] was a mind-bending challenge. ... [D]ue to the pandemic, these classes were held virtually, so having them feel the instrument was not possible. Thus, I was restricted to teaching using just one of the five senses: aural communication. However, I wasn't about to let this unexpected limitation change what, for me, is the most important principle of pedagogy: teachers must always remain open to learning from their students. ... I soon understood that the restrictions, which at first were a challenge, also were a guide. I realized that since all I could teach in this instance was what I could communicate aurally, I should focus on the principles of clear conceptual communication and strong word choice. I described the shape of the instrument in relation to objects that they would already be familiar with and listed a number of words in advance that I wanted to use when explaining how to play the instrument. Most importantly ... I brought [sample] recordings of the great trombonists ... and prepared to play live on my own trombone for the students. Thus, as my lesson took shape, it became much more focused on what the instrument sounds like and is used for, with less emphasis on what it looks like.
>
> This lesson turned out to be very successful, with students in the school referring back to it in later classes and asking further questions about this new instrument. But the individual who learned the most from that lesson ... was me. In all my late nights in the week prior, planning a lesson in which I introduce an instrument to students who could neither see nor feel it ... I realized that an instrument is not the physical material that is shaped to form [it]. ... [It's] only an instrument because of the music it creates, and the emotion it elicits. ... [T]eaching this lesson to these students ... taught me a new way of looking at something I had accepted as fact for a majority of my life. More than this, ... it opened my eyes to a new approach to education,

particularly in our public schools. Students with "disabilities" are often excluded, and teachers may struggle to meet the needs of classes with diverse groups of learners.

My experience teaching this lesson showed me the ... need for a "curb-cut" effect to education. If lessons are designed to be accessible to all types of learners, including those who are labeled as "disabled," the entire class will benefit, and the educational standard will be raised. ... Through an experience teaching abroad, I hope to expand my teaching ability by working with students of a different background, remaining focused on the goal of having the skill necessary to create an inclusive classroom throughout my career.[13]

Leo's "dilemma or crisis" consisted of being "tasked with introducing the trombone to five or six elementary school students, none of whom could see the instrument." The principle he relies upon to surmount what seems like an insuperable challenge is what he describes as the "most important principle of pedagogy: teachers must always remain open to learning from their students."

Below is an exercise to give your students some practice using one of the five inspirational formulas noted above. They should think about how to frame a pivotal moment that will show their readers why and what they care about and therefore how the fellowship will enable them to build upon their insights.

EXERCISE: "ONCE I WAS ... NOW I AM ..."

Draft an essay that employs the organizing principle expressed by "Once I was ... Now I am ..."

Before you start drafting sentences or paragraphs, you may just want to jot down some notes about what your essay will focus on. Remember, the idea is to write about yourself at two different moments in time. ("Now" doesn't literally have to mean "now," just "at a significantly later point in time than 'once.'") You may well want to identify a third moment that represents the turning point along your way from "once" to "now."

Consider how you want to organize your essay. Will you begin with "once" and tell your story in chronological order? Will you begin with "now" and go back in time?

Don't worry about any of this! The most important thing is to just draft freely—and to write about yourself at two different moments in time.

I recommend that your students try one of the five formulas above to begin their personal statement if they feel stuck at first. As they embellish their essays, they may find that they abandon or drift from strict adherence to the propositions they began with, but the formulas are highly useful points of embarkation.

IDENTIFY THE BRIDGE

Finally, another way to begin is with the bridge, that part of the personal statement that links what's personal and what's intellectual. Here it helps to brainstorm. Ask your student to recall situations in which they've found themselves confronted by a dilemma of some kind, by a personal, moral, or political realization, or by the object of their intellectual mission. A scene or anecdote that epitomizes the problem they want to solve is often a promising way to express their motive for undertaking the project they propose to carry out during their fellowship.

Think back to the memorable example of Demi Moore in Chapter 4, who begins her personal statement in dramatic fashion by explaining why her parents gave her such a recognizable name. The last third of that opening paragraph transitions to the bridge, where she reflects on the "happy accident" of her birth and how capricious fortune can be in determining who experiences "justice, fairness, and equality." This is the issue that defines her intellectual mission as she enters law school. This sort of pivot, from an opening "who am I?" to "what I want to do," creates the most common form of the narrative arc in the personal statement. In the example below, one of my students writes about the gulf between what she thought of as the reductionist assumptions built into the reasoning of academic economists and her personal experience, which defied examples she encountered in her textbooks and teachers' lectures:

> In the study of economics, models are often crafted in simplified ways, under a number of broad assumptions. It's not uncommon for an introductory course to ask you to consider an economy in which only apples and oranges are produced, or cars and steel. Conceptual clarity is privileged over the complexities of actual production and consumption. We assume that people are perfectly rational, have all of the information they need, and can weigh it accordingly to make the most optimal decisions. When I first began studying economics, I wondered who these models could ever really apply to, for the world is far more complex than apples and oranges or cars and steel.[14]

After describing how introductory economics seemed counter-intuitive and simplistic, she offers the example of her own parents' superstitions to counter the *homo economicus* theorizing of her economics professors. In the excerpt from her essay that appears below, the bridge appears shaded in gray:

> Growing up, I was taught never to whistle indoors. Such behavior would offend the *domovoi*, a Dobby-like creature in Slavic paganism that embodies the spirit of the hearth, who might run off with all your money. My parents had moved our family to the United States when I was an infant. They characterized living in Russia by its profound *lack*—food shortages, long lines, and inescapable dearth. Having seen the lengths that people will go to in the midst of scarcity, my parents' implicit message to me was: "look out for yourself first." I carried this advice and their experience with me like a shield. It became a complex for me to be able to prove how much I was capable of getting done on my own—how much I had done away with any need to rely on others. It took me many years to realize the harm this did to my relationships with my peers. In the brambles of my own defense mechanisms, I saw conversations as debates to be won rather than an opportunity for new insights. I realized that though I am the product of my history and I carry the stories of those that came before me, each subsequent generation lives in a context that is unprecedented for their ancestors, and not every lesson will be transferable. Looking back on the stories I grew up with, I find my parents straddling the line between a mistrust of others and an inherent sense of whimsy with the animistic ideas that linger in our culture. Even in the story of the *domovoi*, there's an element of playfulness in the mischievous quality of this being. However, beneath the whimsy is a cautionary tale: a world where nothing could be taken for granted, urging one to consider whether they can ever *really* afford to find joy in the present moment.

This lengthy middle portion of her personal statement leads to her intellectual mission—the study of scarcity in developing economies. But along the way she explores the harmful effects of a seemingly innocuous superstition, through which she comes to equate scarcity with mistrust, and selfishness, ultimately, with joylessness. Note, that here the bridge is placed about halfway through the essay, connecting her insight into the implications of her upbringing ("Looking back on the stories I grew up with …") to her intellectual mission ("My goal as an economist …"). The "personal" part of her personal statement forms a "causeway," in effect joining her ideational puzzlement in the first paragraph to the declaration of her ambition as a future economist to understand the economic, social, and personal consequences of scarcity in ways that align intuitively:

> When we apply economics to the lives we lead, many of our presupposed models do not hold. People are not perfectly rational, their information is limited and filtered through the lens of their lived experience and subjective biases. Though I grew up in America, I saw firsthand in my upbringing how difficult it is to unlearn the survival mechanisms you hone living in a developing country. My goal as an economist is to use these insights to find commonalities with people facing poverty. Though cultural practices may at first appear irrational, they are driven by the same instincts that drive our own behaviors. Our personal inexperience with the way these practices manifest does not erase their hold on people's lives; and their pervasiveness suggests that they hold some value in organizing people around a cause. Before proposing interventions to alleviate the weight of poverty, it's vital to understand how poverty shapes a people, and how to bridge the gap between yourself and them.

If your student begins writing an essay by drafting the bridge, after they've drafted it and the biographical portion of their essays, they should ask themselves whether they really see "themselves" in what they've written. They might then ask an intimate, such as a family member or longtime friend, whether the biographical narrative describes the person they know them to be. The bridge should clearly express their motive for the intellectual mission they propose and link it back to who they are and where they come from. If, however, their story, plus the bridge, overshadows the rest of the essay, then they might consider pushing its more personal details into the background. Many students I've worked with often err in the other direction, however, leaving out so much of themselves that they become almost unrecognizable as the authors of their own personal statements. They are so focused on the intellectual mission or the cause that inspires it that the "person" becomes generic, unconvincing, unmemorable.

In the next chapter we'll examine the importance of revision by comparing the early and final drafts of personal statements written by a recent Rhodes Scholar to demonstrate how essays can be transformed when the author thinks hard about what's at stake for them in the opportunity they're seeking.

NOTES

1. The majority of insights relayed in this chapter are drawn from the writing workshops that Margaret A. Sabin and I have been developing since 2016 at Hunter College.
2. Harry Bauld, *On Writing the College Application Essay: The Key to Acceptance at the College of Your Choice* (New York: Collins Reference, 2012), 49.
3. Bauld, *On Writing the College Application Essay*, 56–61.
4. John McPhee, *Draft No. 4: On the Writing Process* (New York: Farrar, Straus and Giroux, 2017). But note that the passages I cite in this chapter are from the essays

as they originally appeared in two issues of *The New Yorker* in 2013. Marie Ponsot and Rosemary Deen, *Beat Not the Poor Desk; Writing: What to Teach, How to Teach It, and Why* (Portsmouth, NH: Boynton/Cook Publishers, 1982).
5. John McPhee, "Draft No. 4," *New Yorker*, April 29, 2013, 33.
6. McPhee, "Draft No. 4," 32.
7. McPhee, "Draft No. 4," 32.
8. McPhee, "Draft No. 4," 32.
9. John McPhee, "Structure," *New Yorker*, January 14, 2013, 49.
10. Ponsot and Deen, chaps. 7–8 in *Beat Not the Poor Desk*. See especially page 101, where Ponsot and Deen provide an overview of their essay "shapes." Note that we have adopted or adapted four of their shapes and added another, "One the one hand, _____. On the other hand, _____." The following section was developed by Margaret Sabin for our workshop at Hunter College.
11. I say "we" here because these examples are drawn from the writing workshop mentioned above.
12. Note, too, that Shahawy's essay employs *both* the "Once/Now" shape proposed by Ponsot and Deen and the "essential elements" of the personal statement that I discuss in Chapter 5.
13. Peter Leo, Fulbright application, September 2021.
14. Anna Vera, personal statement, final draft, written for "Framing Yourself: Writing the Personal Statement for Nationally Competitive Fellowships," Hunter College, Summer Session, May–July, 2022.

WORKS CITED

Bauld, Harry. *On Writing the College Application Essay: The Key to Acceptance at the College of Your Choice*. New York: Collins Reference, 2012.

McPhee, John. "Structure." *New Yorker*, January 14, 2013.

McPhee, John. "Draft No. 4." *New Yorker*, April 29, 2013.

McPhee, John. *Draft No. 4: On the Writing Process*. New York: Farrar, Straus and Giroux, 2017.

Ponsot, Marie, and Rosemary Deen. *Beat Not the Poor Desk: Writing: What to Teach, How to Teach It, and Why*. Portsmouth, NH: Boynton/Cook Publishers, 1982.

Chapter 7

Revising and Ending: Helping Your Students Understand the Importance of Refining Their Personal Statements

REVISE, REVISE, REVISE

Your students should begin where they must but leave plenty of time to step away from their essays to "squint" at them before returning to rearrange paragraphs, clean up sentences, think judiciously about word choice, and get their personal statements under the word count.[1] What follows is a comparison of later and earlier essay drafts by an applicant who ultimately won the Rhodes Scholarship. His early essay drafts for another scholarship documented his mounting accomplishments and growing sense of mastery during his college career. But subsequent drafts for the Rhodes Scholarship ultimately produced a sharpened sense of purpose. In this example, we will read first the opening passage of the candidate's final draft for the Rhodes to demonstrate the development between where he *landed* and where he began. The second example, which is drawn from an essay he submitted for a scholarship with an earlier deadline, illustrates the contrast between the two essays.

Devashish Basnet, whose family were political asylees from Nepal, began one of his major essays with the scene that greeted him late in the summer of 2019 when he worked as an intern for the International Rescue Committee, at one of its shelters for immigrants on the Arizona–Mexico border. The work was charged with meaning, for two years before, the US government had suspended the rights of refugees to claim asylum status and infamously had begun separating children from their parents at the southern border of the United States. But for Basnet, his responsibilities were doubly poignant. When he was just six years old, his own family had escaped life-threatening political oppression in Nepal and come to Queens, New York, by way of India and Amsterdam. When he typed the opening lines of his personal statement, he knew what it felt like to be a supplicant, dependent on the good will of people whose job it was to assist the dispossessed:

> One by one, migrants stepped off the bus and into the scorching heat of the Arizona desert sun. A mosaic of furrowed brows, squinted eyes, and anxious

Figure 7.1 Rhodes Scholar Devashish Basnet, Hunter College, 2023. Photograph by the author

expressions appeared before me and the employees of a shelter that the International Rescue Committee (IRC) had opened to support asylum-seekers arriving at the US–Mexico border. Cutting through all the noise and commotion—from family reunifications, crying toddlers, rosary prayers, and the smell of that day's lunch—tortillas and arroz con frijoles—"Gerardo" and his family took a seat on the folding chairs set up across from me. As I handed a stack of documents to his parents, he quickly intervened and took them out of my hands. In that moment, we shared a mutual understanding. Gerardo, who was seventeen and seeking asylum with his family from Guatemala, appeared frustrated, as he tried his best to act as a translator for his parents who spoke even less English than him.

As an intern with the IRC at the Southern border, I conducted legal orientations for families and witnessed the failure of US immigration policies and the effects of family separation. Talking to Gerardo transported me back to my own experience being processed by the same system he was about to navigate. Was I to warn him about the years he would spend guiding his own family through immigration applications and court hearings, like I had? I saw myself in him; his story paralleling mine. Our two migration stories from opposite sides of the world were connected by a shared paradigm of forced displacement.[2]

REVISING AND ENDING

Compare that beginning with an early draft of the essay Basnet wrote for another nationally competitive fellowship with an earlier deadline:

> After winning the Jeannette K. Watson Fellowship early in my college career, I was given the funding to travel and work at the US–Mexico border with the International Rescue Committee whom I had been working with the entire summer in their New York City headquarters. When I arrived, I was promoted to serving as a shelter coordinator for my previous efforts managing logistics for a small team back in New York. Here in Phoenix, alongside a local staff member, I facilitated trainings, workshops, and culturally competent information sessions to prepare a team of volunteers to support families seeking asylum. I worked to physically prepare the space for the vulnerable migrants that came through our door and helped them to access social services and critical resources. Immediately identifying issues within our processing systems, I began to work diligently with other staff members to strategize around how we could implement changes to streamline inputting data. When I was building out the strategic plan, I realized that we needed to expand the shelter programs in a sustainable way. Our shelter could hold up to 300 families, but it was not enough at the height of the influx of people streaming in from the border.
>
> We needed more room, space, and beds for people. Therefore, I knew we had to start a public campaign for the Airbnb Open Homes Program to come to Arizona. This program was something I heard of and supported back in New York and I saw huge potential for its launch in Arizona. Specifically, the program seeks to connect with homeowners and use their existing Airbnb properties to provide temporary free housing for newly arrived asylum-seeking families who are awaiting adjudication in the United States. I envisioned a robust and dynamic partnership between the program and our shelter and therefore was given the opportunity to pitch the Airbnb Open Homes Program to my boss at the shelter which led to a later pitch of the shelter to Airbnb. The company wanted to see the shelter to better understand the situation on-the-ground, assess the conditions, and understand the urgency of the migration crisis. Spearheading this project, I brought together different stakeholders to advance this private–public partnership. Understanding how these two realms can come together for social good is something I am keen on exploring more, and although it was just a pilot program, I saw its value in setting up in Phoenix and I advocated for it.[3]

Like many applicants I work with, Basnet's earlier draft (the second example here), though competently written, read like a narration of his résumé: a thicket of detail about projects, teams, inputs, stakeholders, campaigns, strategic plans, pitches, and partnerships assembled to persuade his readers of his effectiveness, leadership, and professionalism. His first draft used 50% more words to sketch out the drama that unfolds so memorably in the final version of his later application essay; and what he eventually molded into a vivid tableau had at first been a comparatively airless scene of corporate activity: no smells, sounds, or sensations; no babies crying, aromas wafting, no punishing heat. He converts the rhetoric of decision-makers and policy implementation into a terse but empathic, face-to-face exchange with an immigrant teenager only a year or two younger than himself. In other words, he breathes life and meaning into the *personal* part of the personal statement. Note, finally, that Basnet inserts his bridge at the very beginning of his essay, where he writes, "One by one, migrants stepped off the bus." His first two paragraphs sketch out the problem he wants to tackle. In the second paragraph he turns to his own story and his connection to the young man whose family he is trying to help. From there it is but a step away from his intellectual mission, which is to study world migration and its many causes. And notice how Basnet substitutes the more conventional "Who are you?" beginning of his personal statement, *A*, for *B*, an introduction that begins with the bridge, i.e., his motivation for wanting to study migration patterns internationally. Rather than the more predictable sequence,

A: Who are you? →
B: What motivates you? →
C: What is your intellectual mission →
D: Why do you need this fellowship?

he organizes his essay as follows:

B: What motivates you? →
A: Who are you? →
C: What is your intellectual mission? →
D: Why do you need this fellowship?

BEFRIEND THE WORD COUNT

Most writers of fellowship applications rage at the word count. If the word count is 500 words, they think, "If only it were 750." If it is 750, they think, "if only it were 1,000." Your students shouldn't fight the word count; they should embrace it. If they think of the word count as making their essay, in a sense, like poetry, which imposes arbitrary rules such as meter, structure, and rhythm, forcing writers to bend their words to fit the frame of the form, they can make the word count into an ally. The word count is an undeniable contrivance. But if your students think of the word count as a device that can produce economy and grace, rather than an obstacle, it can help them make tough choices with less worrying of the bone.

Figure 7.2 Sajida Ahmed, Hunter College, 2023. Photograph by the author

To get started, of course, they just need to write—so tell them to sweep the word count aside and unleash themselves from constraint. But once they have a critical mass of words that needs more shape, they can begin tucking in ragged sentences or paragraphs that wander away; they can be unkind to a favorite phrase or sentence. Must every list contain three examples? Does every noun and verb require a modifier? Do they really need that paragraph or is it redundant or distracting? Would the meaning of their essay be any different without it? Most of us, when we draft, use five or six words in a phrase when three will not only suffice but do better. Economize. Pruning creates a clean, direct line between subject and verb, between intention and goal. Eliminating words can feel harder than writing the first draft, so a student should turn an essay over to a trusted reader when they're struggling to get under the word count. Someone who knows them and what they're trying to accomplish can be more steely-eyed about their prose. Their "trusted reader" hasn't invested the time, thought, and grief into composing all those sentences, so they can help the writer dispose of unnecessary words, phrases, sentences, and even paragraphs without remorse. Counsel your students to approach the word count as a helpful tool rather than a confining cage.

ENDING: "TELL ME WHY"

Unlike most forms of essay writing, the conclusion to a personal statement has a distinct purpose, which is for the applicant to make the case for why a fellowship committee should choose *them* over other candidates. This should not be a summary regurgitation of everything they've already said but a persuasive, ideally pithy, final argument that tells the reader *why* they should win the fellowship. Every application *implicitly* asks why they need the experience the fellowship would make possible. Sometimes this question is posed in the negative at the end of an interview: "What will you do if you *do not* win this fellowship?" Or the reverse: "You've gone to the trouble of applying, so make your case: why do you need this?" It is the elephant in the room. A student's answer—likely a version of the same response every other thoughtful candidate will offer—will vary, of course, depending on the nature of the fellowship. For fellowships with a specific purpose (like studying a language) most of the answer is straightforward: the student needs to improve their language proficiency in a country where the language is spoken natively, and perhaps their desire for fluency is connected to their future career. Other fellowships (like the Schwarzman Scholarship, for example) offer a unique curricular element, and the student's reason will involve some combination of the educational experience and the peer group they will be joining and contributing to, which will create a vital intellectual and professional network for them. Still others (e.g., the Rhodes, Marshall, Luce, and Knight-Hennessy) furnish the intellectual and cultural capital that will make possible a much bigger, more ambitious life than they would experience otherwise. Their answer here would be some combination of the particular scholars they hope to work with, the quality of their peers, and the exposure to ideas and people who flow through the most renowned universities in the world that they would encounter by virtue of the fellowship. But of course, each of these answers leaves unspoken the extrinsic rewards that every fellowship offers, advantages that are not to be underestimated but, obviously, need no mentioning.

When I remarked that "most of the answer is straightforward," what I omitted was the signal component of a student's response to this question. In a personal statement, what *persuades* are those qualities that reinforce the readers' sense that the applicant will make a difference in the world and demonstrate their special worthiness. So somewhere in the personal statement, usually toward the end, the student will want to reflect on what winning the fellowship would mean, concretely, for their lives, for their futures, and their ability to pursue something so single-mindedly. When a foundation bestows its award on your student, it enables that student to accomplish something not only for themselves but for others. The most powerful essays often are able to explain not only the candidate's investment in the particular intellectual puzzle they are trying to solve but how their work will improve the lives of others. Thus, ideally, the student will convey something key about their character or commitments that speaks to the committee's belief that awarding the fellowship to *them* rather than someone else will improve the world and may one day even bring honor to the foundation itself.

As I've already intimated, many of the students I work with worry that they may fail to accomplish what they want to undertake when they apply for a fellowship. Indeed, they can't even imagine what might be possible for them and are unused to "dreaming out loud." Allergic to the appearance of pretension, they avoid ambitious claims, however speculative. Therefore, as writers of personal statements who are required to put down on paper the best possible version of what they hope to achieve, they are often wracked with anxiety about falling short. What if their plans change and they don't or can't carry out what they propose? I remind them that while it needs to be true while they're proposing it, this doesn't mean their plans can't change. I remind them that if, in the course of their plan of study or in conducting research, they change what they want to study or accomplish, they need to respect the process.

Just because they set out on one path and veer onto another doesn't make them disingenuous or indecisive; it can simply reflect an honest response to different ways of looking at the same problem. It's easy to get locked into the "mission" they set out on and forget to allow for their own unfolding or changing perspective. The personal statement of a twenty-year-old, moreover, has a shorter shelf life than the personal statement of a fifty-year-old person. At twenty, they're still growing and becoming who they will be as a fully formed adult thinker. And while they need to express concretely what they can achieve by winning a fellowship, in the end the whole enterprise is about *possibility*: what can they make possible, and what's possible for them to become? The personal statement is not a contract. It is an articulation of the applicant's plan of action based on an intellectual puzzle they're trying to solve, and a projection of where they expect their commitments will take them. Unlike a grant application in which their sole objective is to describe a problem they are attempting to solve, they are not forever bound to the personal statement.[4]

In this respect, I am again reminded of Agnes Callard's distinction between "self-cultivation" and "aspiration" as the means by which one's values are nurtured. "Self-cultivation" is a commitment to change one's behavior in order to achieve something they believe in or know is good, whereas "aspiration" is a striving to find something, which though "blurry," comes into focus while "finding it." A research plan for a fellowship application is more like self-cultivation in the sense that, having outlined a goal based on a value, judgment, or research objective for which they set out to gather evidence, they hope to "prove" the rectitude of the mission that informs it. However, the best research plan is open-ended and "aspirational" in the sense that in carrying it out one seeks to understand a phenomenon knowing that, in the seeking, one's understanding will deepen and expand, leading to new and important insights along the way.

If your student changes their mind or changes course, no one will be coming to ask them for their money back. So in *this* sense the plan they propose in the fellowship application only needs to be true while they're conceiving it. Fellowship committees expect their recipients to continue developing, thinking, evolving. All that matters is that the aspirations they express genuinely reflect their intentions and that they commit themselves fully to enacting them. Your students shouldn't worry, then, that they're being inauthentic somehow if later something rearranges their sense of purpose or their opinion changes. Because each fellowship is created for a different reason, their missions vary and, consequently, so do their emphases: some fully stress academic or intellectual excellence; others look for a demonstration of past and a projection of future leadership; still others insist on the importance of openness, exploration, and growth. This means that the personal statement for each fellowship will be tailored to its specific mission. The effort a student puts into composing a personal statement should yield a basic template for other personal statements: there's nothing inauthentic about a student's altering the components of the draft they begin with. The "autobiographical" part of a personal statement may remain unaltered (though the writer may add to it or subtract from it, depending on the fellowship), but the impetus for action and the student's plea for "why they need this" may change significantly for different applications and even reshape the intellectual mission.

This actually happened to me when I was formulating my dissertation topic in graduate school. I was interested in the changing texture of parent–child relations in the US working class during the first third of the twentieth century. Schooling, I knew, was a part of the explanation for this change, but when I applied for a fellowship designed for scholars interested in education-related topics, I was forced to think harder about the role of schooling in the phenomenon I was researching and realized that it was actually much more important than I had previously appreciated. It shifted the way I thought about my subject and caused me to probe this aspect of my argument much more deeply than I would have otherwise. Similarly, the kind of "stretching" of purpose and aims that a fellowship application can require of students if they are to fit the terms of particular fellowships can, in fact, amend and sharpen the student's intellectual mission, changing the way they think about the problem they're trying to solve. This can be a healthy and authentic way to evolve one's scope and purpose as an intellectual, activist, or leader. It can signify growth and reflection.[5] And this is why winning a fellowship, while exhilarating, is secondary to making the effort, which will cultivate deeper understanding and move your student forward in their quest, however they conceive it.

REVISING AND ENDING

FINAL THOUGHTS

The format of virtually every personal statement of course varies with every application. Some specify areas for discussion the applicant *must* address, others are entirely open-ended. They tend to range from 750 to 1,500 words. To give your students a sense of the variation (and consistency) of the prompts of major fellowship application essays, I've reproduced examples of prompts from a handful of scholarships:

1. Candidates should describe their academic and other interests and pursuits.
2. Provide a short Personal Statement describing your academic and other interests. This statement should describe the specific area of proposed study and your reasons for wishing to study at _____.
3. Use Personal Statement to convey a sense of who you are, and reflect on, among other things, (a) your personal journey; (b) your long-range professional interests, and how they have developed; (c) how you have embodied your own kind of leadership; and (d) how a year in _____ might be transformative.
4. Write about your Personal Background; your Intellectual Merit; the Broader Impact of your Research and your Future Goals.
5. A statement of 1,000 words or less from the nominee devoted to describing their research or creative interests for graduate study and career aspirations beyond these studies. It should also include a discussion of the most relevant academic, professional, extracurricular, and personal experiences that have influenced or shaped the nominee's plans.

If they aim to compose a personal statement of about 1,000 words, your students will have an essay they can customize for virtually any application. Some applications will require them to "break out" portions of their essays to address qualities a particular fellowship emphasizes, such as leadership, or commitment to public service, enhancing relations between two nations, or addressing the problems of the twenty-first century. Others provide intentionally broad prompts to see whether, given only general instructions, the applicant will address the values the fellowship articulates in its mission statement or items they list in their selection criteria. A coherent, well-formed, and authentic personal statement can be lengthened or trimmed according to the purposes of whatever scholarship your student is applying for. In the writing of it they will have articulated who they are, what matters to them, what they're good at, and what they have to offer the world—whether that "world" is their particular academic discipline or the most remote parts of the Earth.

EXERCISE: A FIVE-YEAR PLAN FOR FELLOWSHIP APPLICATIONS

Scholarships and fellowships for which I'm eligible, by year.

YEAR ONE

Internal (college):

_____
_____

External/national:

_____
_____

YEAR TWO

Internal (college):

_____
_____
_____

External/national:

_____
_____
_____

YEAR THREE

Internal (college):

_____
_____
_____

External/national:

_____
_____
_____

YEAR FOUR

Internal (college):

_____
_____
_____
_____

External/national:

_____
_____
_____
_____

YEAR FIVE

Internal (college):

_____
_____
_____
_____

External/national:

_____
_____
_____
_____
_____
_____

EXERCISE: WHERE DO YOU SEE YOURSELF IN 5 YEARS? ... IN 10 YEARS? ... 15 YEARS?

Describe your future self at three moments in time, each 5 years apart, with the first being 5 years after you graduate from college. Who do you hope to be 5, 10, and 15 years after you graduate? What do you hope to have achieved in your chosen career?

> **EXERCISE: REFLECTION ON THE RELATIONSHIP BETWEEN FELLOWSHIPS AND POST-BACCALAUREATE EDUCATION AND PROFESSIONAL PREPARATION**
>
> 1. What do you expect to accomplish with your fellowship, and how will the experience help you achieve your long-term goals?
> 2. What will you do after graduating if you do not receive a fellowship?

NOTES

1. For a really fine essay on revising, see John McPhee, "Draft No. 4," *New Yorker*, April 29, 2013, 32–38.
2. Devashish Basnet, final draft, personal statement, Rhodes Scholarship, September 2021.
3. Devashish Basnet, early draft, leadership essay, Summer 2021.
4. For good examples of the differences between a fellowship application and a grant proposal (specifically, to support research in the sciences or social sciences), see chaps. 3–7 in Andrew J. Friedland, Carol L. Folt, and Jennifer L. Mercer, eds., *Writing Successful Science Proposals* (New Haven, CT: Yale University Press, 2018).
5. Agnes Callard, "Liberal Education and the Possibility of Valuational Progress," *Social Philosophy & Policy*, 34, no. 2 (Winter 2017): 18.

WORKS CITED

Callard, Agnes. "Liberal Education and the Possibility of Valuational Progress." *Social Philosophy & Policy*, 34, no. 2 (Winter 2017): 1–22.

Friedland, Andrew J., Carol L. Folt, and Jennifer L. Mercer, eds. *Writing Successful Science Proposals*. New Haven, CT: Yale University Press, 2018.

McPhee, John. "Draft No. 4." *New Yorker*, April 29, 2013, 32–38.

Conclusion: Recruiting, Cultivating, and Retaining Student Talent, and Faculty Collaboration

For many of us, helping students understand the nature of the personal statement is the defining activity of our work with fellowship applicants. This is truer, on average, I know, at large public universities than at highly selective colleges where much of this work occurs in the context of engaged faculty mentoring. At institutions like mine, where there are rarely too many applicants for the number of nominations allotted for the most illustrious scholarships, the primary challenge is recruiting sufficient numbers of qualified applicants for all the opportunities available. So I'd like to conclude by offering some suggestions about how to attract and cultivate student talent on your campus and how to enlist faculty in the effort.

FELLOWSHIP ADVISING AND LIBERAL EDUCATION

As elite institutions began to diversify their campuses during the last three decades, they quietly (and slowly) evolved their approach to advising students as well.[1] While formerly administrators assumed that every student admitted, if pointed in the direction of the institution's ample support services, should be able to thrive, by the 2010s the ethos of academic guidance began to shift. Because there was a superabundance of help available to students in every subject area and at every level of difficulty, the prevailing attitude before the last decade was that it was the student's responsibility to take advantage of it. Too frequently, perhaps, we failed to understand the obstacles—psychological, cultural, and material—that prevented struggling students from utilizing what help there was and held them strictly accountable when they didn't.[2]

For advisors, this philosophical reorientation requires greater effort and imagination as well as judicious sensitivity to the individual student's needs.[3] The implication for us, as fellowship advisors, is that we owe it to our students to be more entrepreneurial about including them in the fellowship application process as well. But it also introduces an unprecedented opportunity: to

DOI: 10.4324/9781003455387-8

conceive of the fellowship application process as a complementary curriculum within a liberal education, as each occasion to apply for a fellowship offers each student a chance for self-reflection, goal-setting, skills building, intellectual development, cultivation of a sense of purpose, and overall growth.

Yet, whether you're at Harvard or at Hunter, even if you see the value of involving as many students as you can in the fellowship application process, you may feel that you're not reaching every student you might, because you're struggling to engage them "on their terms."[4] For reasons explored in this book but not fully comprehensible to us, many of our students just don't see themselves as viable fellowship candidates or they calculate that the effort expended wouldn't be worth the time, energy, and emotional investment needed to be competitive. Again, we've only recently awakened to the enormous potential of students whose families are new to college and bring formerly underappreciated, untapped talent and perspective to the pool of students we've been accustomed to working with. But there is another broad, seemingly undifferentiated group of students on all of our campuses whose potential also often goes unnoticed. So inured are we to listening for the student who has prevailed in the face of long odds that we run the risk of missing those silently motoring through their courses toward graduation. These students can appear as ordinary to us as they do to themselves. Still, we are in the business of discernment; and while difficult, we owe it to our students to be vigilant about being open to *all* of them all the time—attuned to the subtlety of minute variation in the ways they present themselves. When we look past a student who appears unexceptional, we only reinforce their reluctance to seek us out, while depriving ourselves of discovering how interesting and full of promise that young person may really be.

What I'm suggesting is that we extend our resolve to create a more equitable academic experience to those students we too readily assume are equipped with the cultural and social capital needed to compete for fellowships, were they so inclined. These are high-achieving students of various social and ethnic backgrounds, who, with a little encouragement, would contemplate applying for a scholarship. So, our task is twofold: to find ways to engage as many students as we can and to look carefully for the thing that sets each student apart from their peers. Since we're trained to do the latter, the chief difficulty is to find ways of involving students ordinarily invisible to ourselves and students who, in turn, feel themselves to be invisible. How then, can we overcome these challenges?

THE "HAIL MARY" PASS THAT BECAME PART OF MY PLAYBOOK

When I was hired to establish a fellowships office at Hunter just twelve weeks before the next fellowships cycle kicked off, my mission was to find the fastest route to identifying viable candidates for applications that were due by mid-September. While I was able to get lists of email addresses for high-achieving students in the College's honors programs, I suspected that the surest approach might be to meet with any student who had already won a smaller scholarship—either a fellowship for language study abroad or some kind of internal departmental prize. I scoured the school's website for fellowship announcements and visited the websites of individual departments to "scrape" the names of student award-winners from the previous spring, and contacted every one of the students listed. One of these students became Hunter's first-ever Marshall Scholar. Gathering the names of student winners from my college's website has remained a staple of my recruiting practices each year.

Because your institution is different from mine in ways only you can appreciate, I won't presume to suggest which assortment of recruitment strategies will work best at yours. But there is one exception: the most effective strategy for identifying and recruiting the hardest-to-reach student is the faculty referral. You know this, but if you're like me you may need to remind yourself that students' teachers have the best sense of their potential because they are reading their work, observing them in class or in lab, conversing with them in office hours, and grading their exams. They are constantly measuring them against their peers, so they form strong impressions of student potential in terms of their ability to express themselves verbally and in writing, of their analytical ability, intellectual curiosity, and capacity to work hard. When a teacher takes the trouble to relay the names of students who have performed particularly well in one of their courses and you can use their endorsement in an email to the student asking them to meet with you, *nothing* is so effective in getting students to follow through.

Still, involving faculty in your mission is its own challenge. They are busy, can be hard to reach, or simply reluctant about going the extra mile to help you when they have to be so singularly focused on teaching, committee work, research, and publication. The culture of your institution can engender an appreciative, indifferent, or decidedly ambivalent attitude toward your work by faculty—I have experienced all three. Much of your institution's culture is idiosyncratic and arises from the politics of your college or university, department, or scholarly discipline. Nonetheless, you're bound to find support among some small group of faculty initially, and it's important to nurture these relationships because they will pay off mightily over the years. The faculty at my college are essential partners in identifying student talent from year to year. It can be difficult, however, especially at large institutions and especially at commuter schools where faculty tend to spend little time on campus, to cultivate these relationships. Yet, if you are faithful about acknowledging your faculty's role in the success of your students, they will come to value you, admire your work, and help you develop a talent pipeline that will sweep up those students who might otherwise obscure themselves. The more you make the faculty a part of your mission, the more likely it is that a handful of allies will grow into a chorus of supporters.

At the risk of stating the obvious, I want to mention a couple of practices I employ to keep these referrals flowing from year to year. The first pertains to recruiting faculty and the second to sustaining these critical relationships. I've been invited to speak with division deans, department heads, and at faculty meetings. For me, at least, these pleas to faculty to refer their high-performing students yield very little if they are not followed up by emails to the individuals who attend. Even more fruitful, I've found, is writing to faculty about a student for whom they have already written a letter of recommendation. At the end of every year, you have a bank of faculty names accumulated from the most recent fellowships cycle. Make a habit of writing a short note to each recommender, both to thank them for taking the time to write for their students and to refer others who have stood out in their classes. This almost always elicits a response. Another source of recruitment are faculty who have served on your mock interview committees. At some institutions, of course, participation in candidate preparation is considered a form of "service" that is expected by department chairs and contributes to the tenure portfolio. At others it is not, yet faculty often do this work out of a sense of commitment to their undergraduates. In either case, a prompt "thank you" afterward and following up with news of the student's success is both appreciated and remembered. This group of faculty, over time, will form a critical mass of support for your work as you involve them in the success of your students and the mission of your office. Moreover, when faculty do take the trouble to send student names your way, let them know that you have met with the student and thank them again for the referral. This tends to keep them coming back to refer more students to you in the future.

THE IMPORTANCE OF WORKING WITH STUDENTS EARLY IN THEIR TIME AT COLLEGE

At public universities, where the opportunities for first- and second-year students are less abundant than at well-resourced institutions, reaching students early is critical to orienting them to the opportunities that await them as juniors and seniors. If you don't involve them during their first two years, for many it's too late. They often haven't the benefit of exposure to work environments that internships provide, research opportunities offered by their professors, or the cultural and personal leavening that study abroad offers, so they haven't the perspective, insight, and understanding needed to identify possible future goals or to formulate ideals that will serve as an internal north star. They lack experience applying for scholarships within reach early on that build the confidence they need to apply for more competitive scholarships later.

You have some obvious partners in this enterprise: again, faculty who have been impressed by students in their first or second year are key to surfacing students who might otherwise elude you over the course of their college careers. Even more consistently reliable are the directors of your college's first- and second-year honors programs, your colleagues who direct your university's pre-law, pre-health, engineering, and business programs, and your study abroad office. Most large public institutions today have some form of honors college that serves its top-ranked students at the point of admission. Working routinely with these students' advisors is obviously the easiest way to tap into talent that has already been recognized and is being actively mentored. I take every opportunity to conduct a general presentation on fellowship opportunities to honors students while in their first two years, after which, I get a steady flow of students as they progress toward graduation. (I also "reintroduce" myself to students newly admitted to honors programs designed for students in their latter two years of college.)

Students (and their parents) identify "pre-professional" programs or majors early, often even before they get to college, and are thus incentivized to seek out the services of pre-law, pre-health, engineering, and business programs within their first or second year of enrollment. Your colleagues who direct these offices will already have formed opinions of their best students and can help you and their students find one another. In this collaborative approach, everyone prospers, as the students' academic experience is enhanced by your engagement with the students you hold in common.

I also work hand-in-glove with my study abroad office. As we're all aware, study abroad scholarships represent the most numerous sources of funding available to undergraduates. Many of these scholarships are accessible to students beginning in their first year of college, and because applicants are required to work with your study abroad programs as a part of their application process, study abroad advisors are natural allies in identifying students motivated to seek your assistance.

Since the pandemic imposed remote learning on every aspect of university life, virtual information sessions have become an invaluable recruiting tool for fellowships offices. At a university that has been a late-adopter of the kind of electronic tools that make identifying students by major, grade point average, progress toward degree, and other characteristics, obtaining this capacity has been a giant leap forward for me. Still, students have to open your email in the first place, and as we all know, they are notoriously poor about responding to email. Nonetheless, it remains the most comprehensive means available to most of us to publicize fellowship opportunities and to invite students *en masse* to our information sessions. Despite its limitations, the virtue of the online information session is its ability to inform large groups of students about potential opportunities.

CONCLUSION

    Undoubtedly, in-person information sessions offer the best connection between your students and the presenter, whether you or the director of a featured fellowship describes its mission. The in-person session makes possible a much more interactive question-and-answer session and gives the representative a finer sense of the talent at your institution. But the in-person session can only reach the students who happen to attend. Whereas in the past, I would get a dozen or so students to attend an information session led by the director of a national fellowship, that same information session offered online today attracts scores of students. This phenomenon may be peculiar to students at commuter schools like my own, and it may, like so much electronic communication, prove evanescent and fade over time in its effectiveness. For now, however, it surpasses in-person information sessions at getting the word out. But imperative in either case is individual follow-up. Most of the online advising tools at our schools allow us to record which students register for and attend our information sessions, so it's possible (though time-intensive) to follow up individually with students who show enough interest to attend your information session and even with those who register but don't or can't attend. Offering them an in-person appointment will almost always get a positive, appreciative response.

    Finally, student organizations offer ideal gatherings to address students who might otherwise never learn about fellowship opportunities, and they are almost endless in number and kind: affinity groups based on student identity, student government, community and public service clubs, political organizations, debating societies, varsity and club sports, newspapers and magazines, orchestras, bands, choral groups, departmental student clubs, theater, dance, fraternities and sororities, and so on. At Ivy League schools, student organizations number in the hundreds, and students often say retrospectively that these organizations were the source of their most meaningful friendships and learning experiences during their college years.[5] These peer-arranged and regulated activities are doubly important on campuses where the opportunities for community-building lack an institutional infrastructure. While the absence of adult involvement is often an attractive feature of many of these groups, when faculty or administrators pay attention to them to discuss special topics, or in the case of fellowship advisors, to talk about possible opportunities, students tend to react enthusiastically.

    Their organizations' goals also frequently align with qualities sought by fellowships, such as leadership, public and community service, "energetic use of talent," concern for others, cultural openness, increasing international understanding, creativity, skill-building, and intellectual curiosity.[6] On those occasions when you're invited to speak to a group in its own space, the in-person presentation of information about scholarships is optimal. You've already demonstrated your interest in their group's activity, you are there specifically for them, and their members are usually required to attend, so you have both a captive and receptive audience. An additional benefit of meeting with student organizations is that, because they have to work extremely hard to attract new members from the first-year class each year and the organizational hierarchy for most groups peaks at junior year, it's a great way to gain exposure to students early in their time at college and in a setting already endorsed by their student "elders." Again, individual follow-up is crucial, but with world enough and time, meeting students in these settings offers your very best chance of connecting with a representative cross-section of students on your campus.

Another approach to promoting the services you make available to all students is to organize panels with student presenters on topics with inherent, if often unarticulated, appeal. The ability to conduct these events online makes broad attendance possible and also facilitates the participation of alumni, who as near-peers familiar with your institution can speak to students with an apt mix of authority and authenticity. In recent semesters I've arranged panel discussions on "imposter syndrome," "how to create mentors," "how to get a lab position," and "how to talk to your professors." These "fellowship-adjacent" discussions attracted hundreds of students—students who might never have attended any of my information sessions, and they each occasioned a brief discussion of the work I do, which allowed me to invite attendees to make individual appointments with me.

Workshops on elements of the personal statement demystify the fellowship application process by breaking it down into steps, explaining its purpose, and demonstrating its broader usefulness in their development. In addition to a non-credit, week-long workshop on composing the personal statement, I offer "stand-alone" workshops throughout the year on "interviewing your parents and understanding yourself"; "connecting-the-dots" (helping students understand the relationship of seemingly disparate activities and commitments to one another); "identifying your values" (what you care about); and "developing a sense of purpose." For students I've previously worked with, I also offer an advanced workshop on revising the personal statement. Each of these workshops helps students gain insight into themselves, their motives for the course of study they've chosen, which fellowships may be appropriate for them at different stages, and exploring potential career paths.

My personal statement writing workshop (and the more in-depth five-week summer course on the same topic) enables students to think hard about all of these issues and leaves them with a first draft of what they can develop into the germ of a personal statement for any number of purposes: fellowship and graduate school applications, even cover letters for future jobs. Yet, as I suggested earlier, there are always some students who will feel, alongside many of their classmates, that their personal story is comparatively mundane. Ordinary in their upbringing—shielded, even, from the trials that many of

CONCLUSION

their peers have endured—they have great difficulty getting at the core of who they are and what they have to offer the world. I urge these students to concentrate on locating the inspiration for whatever aspect of their studies has become a vital activity for them in college. I ask them to meditate on the particular intellectual problem they're trying to untangle.

Whether they are studying astrophysics or sixteenth-century Ottoman art, they need to try to understand the source of the pleasure they get from working out intellectual puzzles. Exploring *its specific nature* will lead them to the motive underlying their reason for wanting to become a scientist or a historian. Was it an image that captivated them in the darkness of an art history lecture hall, when suddenly a series of seemingly disconnected details slid into focus for them? Or was it a childhood affinity for gazing at the night sky that led them to wonder how brown dwarfs can help us understand the structural and dynamic features of the universe? In essence, they need to contemplate their own curiosity. This is, of course, a necessary exercise for all applicants but is especially helpful for students who feel there is nothing remarkable about who they are or where they come from. Each workshop creates a unique occasion for students to get comfortable thinking and talking about their ambitions, reflecting on themselves and their beginnings, for them to know me and me to know them and to nourish their trust. The more and longer I know them and the more they trust me, the better I can guide them and support their future success.

Finally, I'm aware that much of what I have to say about engaging students who routinely elude us has greater relevance for advisors at large public institutions. However, whether you're at a large or small institution, you may be looking for ways to involve students who typically aren't inclined to put themselves forward for fellowships. If so, you might consider some of the initiatives I've described. Collectively, these strategies will help you engage students who formerly wouldn't have thought about applying for fellowships. Further, you'll be able to sync with recent initiatives to diversify the applicant pools of the most notable scholarships while exposing a wider range of students to the scholarship application process. In addition, you'll give more students the chance to develop personally, intellectually, socially, and professionally during their college years.

NOTES

1. I mean "advising" here in the broadest sense of the word; i.e., everything entailed in assuring that students thrive: from who advises them across their four years, to individual and group tutoring, to the emotional, medical, and psychological support available to students, and their "standing" from semester to semester. Efforts to diversify undergraduate applicant pools at selective colleges began in earnest during the 1980s. For the years 1967–2007, see fig. 2 in Caroline Hoxby, "College Choices Have Consequences," *SIEPR Policy Brief* (December 2012), https://citeseerx.ist.psu.edu/

document?repid=rep1&type=pdf&doi=c8c8ea663a36e6143723330f668714915f71ce22. For the past two decades, see the report by the National Center for Education Statistics, "College Enrollment Rates," in *The Condition of Education 2020*, https://nces.ed.gov/programs/coe/pdf/coe_cpb.pdf.
2. My observation on the "shift" in the philosophy of academic advising over the last two decades is based on my experience as a residential college dean at Yale for fourteen years and as Deputy Dean of the College at Brown, where I chaired the Committee on Honors and Academic Standing for six years.
3. See the conclusion to Anthony Abraham Jack, *The Privileged Poor: How Elite Colleges Are Failing Disadvantaged Students* (Cambridge, MA: Harvard University Press, 2019), on the importance of understanding the specific needs of students whose pre-college experience differentiates them from their peers.
4. I want to give special thanks to my colleague Greg Llacer, of Harvard University, for raising this important issue in his critique of an earlier draft of this book.
5. Richard J. Light emphasizes this point as well in chap. 3 of his *Making the Most of College: Students Speak their Minds* (Cambridge, MA: Harvard University Press, 2001), which analyzes "Suggestions from Students" and urges mentors to ask their advisees about the significance of extracurriculars in their overall college experience; see especially pp. 25–34.
6. Goals such as these were identified at the outset of NAFA and are articulated in the mission statements of a range of nationally competitive scholarships. See Alice Stone Ilchman, Warren F. Ilchman, and Mary Hale Tolar, "Strengthening Nationally Competitive Scholarships: Thoughts from an International Conference in Bellagio," in *Beyond Winning: National Scholarship Competitions and the Student Experience*, ed. Suzanne McCray (Fayetteville, AK: University of Arkansas, 2005), 75.

WORKS CITED

Hoxby, Caroline. "College Choices Have Consequences." *SIEPR Policy Brief* (December 2012). https://citeseerx.ist.psu.edu/document?repid=rep1&type=pdf&doi=c8c8ea663a36e6143723330f668714915f71ce22.

Ilchman, Alice Stone, Warren F. Ilchman, and Mary Hale Tolar. "Strengthening Nationally Competitive Scholarships: Thoughts from an International Conference in Bellagio." In *Beyond Winning: National Scholarship Competitions and the Student Experience*, edited by Suzanne McCray. Fayetteville, AK: University of Arkansas, 2005.

Jack, Anthony Abraham. *The Privileged Poor: How Elite Colleges Are Failing Disadvantaged Students*. Cambridge: Harvard University Press, 2019.

Light, Richard J. *Making the Most of College: Students Speak Their Minds*. Cambridge, MA: Harvard University Press, 2001.

National Center for Education Statistics. "College Enrollment Rates." *The Condition of Education 2020*. https://nces.ed.gov/programs/coe/pdf/coe_cpb.pdf.

Index

Page numbers in *italics* refer to figures.

AANAPISI Scholarship 61
academic achievements 81–2
academic degrees 21
academic excellence 23–4
academic experiences 66–7, 81, 108, 111
academic interests 81–2
academic scientists 6
academic success 25
accomplishments 4, 30, 36, 41–2, 47–8, 59, 73, 75
achievements 3, 4, 30, 49, 68; academic 81–2; creating inventory of 35
actions 12, 72–3
activities 28–9, 35–6, 41, 66–7
adaptability 26
adolescence 53–4
advising 107, 114n1
affinity group organizations 28
aims 12, 72–3
ambition 28, 49
anecdotes 61, 69, 70, 91
anxious thoughts 45
application essays 9, 26–7, 32, 62, 65–6, 71–2; beginning 84–93; "bridge" in 70–3, 77, 91–3, 98; ending 100–102; parts of 70, 75, 80; prompts 103; refining 95–102; sample 75–80; "shapes" 87; structuring 69–72, 87–90

application process 4, 22, 108; extrinsic aspects 5–7, 12, 14; as a form of self-understanding 12; intrinsic aspects 4, 7–8, 12, 13; planning 104–6
art 28, 32
aspiration 11–12, 101
attitudes 7
aural communication 89
authenticity 41, 49–50, 52, 68–82, 102

Basnet, Devashish 95–8
Bauld, Harry 84
Beat Not the Poor Desk 85
behavior 7; drivers of 13; impact of our narratives on 45–6
Beinecke Scholarship 19, 21, 69
beliefs 8
belonging 33, 50; *see also* imposter syndrome
biographies 45, 73, 81, 93
brainstorming 91
bridge (in structuring essays) 72, 85, 91–93

Callard, Agnes 11–12, 101
Calarco, Jessica McCrory 15
"calling" 12–13
challenges 28

INDEX

childhood 53–4
civic education programs 28
clubs: leadership 26; membership 28
collaboration 26
college degrees 10
college education 10, 50–1; affordability of 15n2; and occupational security 9; vocational approach to 8; *see also* college degrees; college ranking; college organizations
college organizations 29
college ranking 16n12
commitments 10, 66
community-building 112
community service 28, 36
"competing narratives" 45–47
"connecting the dots" 41, 59, 60–1, 66–7, 81
connections 6–7
creative thinking 33
creativity 26
cultural curiosity 24, 28, 60
cultural interests 36
cultural networks 29
culture 7, 109
current events 24
customs 7

Damon, William 12–14, 32, 82n6
dance 28
Davis-Putter Scholarship 61
debates 11, 28, 29, 61, 92
Deen, Rosemary 85, 87
developmental approach (to writing the personal statement) xv, 108
developmental steps 11, 12
diversity 2, 44, 62–5, 107
Draft No. 4 85
drafts 68–9, 85–90, 93, 95–9, 102; final 87–8, 93, 95; first 85–6, 98, 99, 113; "vomit" 85; *see also* application essays; revision; word count; writing
dreams 43, 44, 46–7

editing 41
egalitarianism 25
Emerging Leaders in Public Service 61
empathy 33, 43
employment 28
energy 28, 29
engagement 28–9
esteem 14
ethnic background 48
exercises: "Connecting the Dots" 66–7, 81; inventory of activities and achievements 35–7, 81–2; "Inventory of Purpose" 14, 32, 81; planning 104–6; writing 40–1, 85, 90
experiences: academic 66–7, 81, 108, 111; applying for fellowships 22; applying for scholarships 34–5; extracurricular 28–9; formative 70, 73; international 7; leadership 22, 26–8; professional 29
extracurricular activities 28–9, 35–6
extrinsic (reasons for applying for fellowships) 5, 12; rewards 14, 29, 100

faculty collaboration 109–10
failure: dealing with 22, 52; "narratives" 45–7, 52
fairness 25
"faking it" 49
families 40–3, 50, 55; immigrant 3, 42, 49, 60, 63; *see also* grandparents; parents; siblings
fellowship advising xv–xviii, 107–8
fellowship committees 24, 27, 33, 47, 49, 58–66, 102
fellowships: definition 2–3, 16n7; post-baccalaureate 34, 48, 106; range of opportunities 3–4; reasons for applying 3–8; rewards of winning 14; *see also* fellowship committees; fellowship advising; scholarships
fiction 24

117

INDEX

first-generation college students (FGCS) 1, 8, 19–20, 25, 64
flexibility 26
flourishing 7, 11, 12
founders (of organizations) 26
formative experiences 70, 73
free associating 84
freewrite 85–6
Fulbright scholarships 19, 59, 89
fulfilment 4

Gable, Rachel 25
Giamatti, Bartlett 9
Gilman scholarship 34
goals 4–5, 8, 10, 13, 26, 32, 45, 48, 60, 65
Goldwater Scholarship 61
Govern For America 61
grade point average 24
grandparents 53
grants 16n7, 101
group study 25
"grousing" 84
growth 5, 26

help-seeking 25
Hicke, Daniel 59
"hidden curriculum" xv, 1, 15n4
Hidden Curriculum, The 25
hobbies 4, 36
honors programs 23
"hooks" 69
humanities disciplines 32
Humanity-in-Action scholarship 31
humility 26, 49

identity 62, 63
immigrant families 3, 42, 60, 63; *see also* first-generation college students (FGCS)
imposter syndrome 46–52
independence 33
independent study 24

information sessions 111–12
initiative 26, 27
injustice 62, 77; "narratives" 45–7
innovation 26
insecurities 49; *see also* imposter syndrome
inspiration 10, 81
Institute for Recruitment of Teachers 61
intellectual curiosity 23–4, 28, 112
intellectual development 24
intellectual mission 32, 40, 60, 68–71, 73–5, 79, 81–2, 92–3, 102
interests 36, 66; academic 81–2
international experiences 7; *see also* study abroad scholarships
international networks 7
internships 3, 4, 6, 23, 28–9, 34, 50, 110
interviews 27; with parents 42–4, 52–5
intrinsic (reasons for applying for fellowships) 7, 12; rewards 4, 13
"Inventory of Purpose" exercise 14, 32, 81
Islam 74–5, 78; *see also* Muslims
Ivy League 112

Jack, Anthony Abraham xxiiin6, 15n4, 115n3
Jeannette K. Watson Fellowship 97
job market 7, 33; *see also* jobs
jobs 4, 43, 54–5; *see also* job market
Johnson, Emily 19–22

Kaplan, Robert Steven 44–7, 52
Knight-Hennesy Scholarship 100

labs 29
language 7; courses 25, 33; heritage learners 33; learning 33, 59, 60; scholarships 24, 100; second 23, 33–4; teachers 34
leaders 26–7, 61–2, 74; "natural" 27; *see also* leadership

INDEX

leadership: of college organizations 29; experience 22, 26–8; forms of 26–7; holistic 26; markers of 26; practicing 28; roles 26; "thought" 27; and underrepresented groups 62; *see also* leaders

learning 26; languages 33, 59, 60; remote 111; from students 89–90

Leo, Peter 89–90

letters: of recommendation 21, 25, 26, 34, 29–31; writing 86

liberal education 10, 11, 107–8

life-course decisions 7

Light, Richard 24, 25

"linkage" 59

literary magazines 26

literature 32

Luce Scholarship 26, 28, 69, 100

luck 22

magazines 26, 32

marriage 54

Marshall Scholarship 26, 69, 100, 109

Marshall-Motley Scholars Program 61

mass education 4

McCray, Suzanne xvi, 56n10

McPhee, John 41, 85–7

meaning, creating 5

medical school applications 72

Mellon Mays Undergraduate Fellowship 61

mentoring xix, 9, 11, 24–6; *see also* mentors

mentors 6–7, 11, 47, 51; identifying 24–6; *see also* mentoring

middle-class 9, 63

Midwest 25

Mock Trial 28, 29

Model Congress 28, 29

Model UN 28, 29

Moore, Demi 63, 70, 91–3

motives 13, 14, 27, 28, 36, 40, 43, 52, 69–70, 72–3, 88, 91, 114

multilingualism 7

"multiplier effect" 6

museums 24

music 28

Muslims 76–8

"narrative arc" 70, 75, 80

narratives: contest between chronology and theme 87; developing 41; "failure" 45–7, 52; "injustice" 45–7; of one's own life 44–7; "success" 45, 46, 52

national perspective 7

National Science Foundation Graduate Research Fellowship 61, 68

New York Times Book Review podcast 24

New York Times Weekly Quiz 24

news 24

newspapers 26, 32, 36

non-fiction 24

Not the Poor Desk 87

office hours 25–6

open-mindedness 26

opinions 7

opportunities 14, 46; orienting students to 110–14

organizations: affinity group 28; college 29; founders of 26; student 26, 112–13

outlining 84

oversharing 65

parents 3, 42–5, 48–9, 52–5, 63

participating 28

passions 9–11, 71–2

Path to Purpose, The 14

Paul & Daisy Soros Fellowship 61

Pauli Murray Fellowship 61

peer advising 28

peer education 28

peers 6, 7, 28

personal growth 5

119

INDEX

personal history 40, 113–14; *see also* biographies
personal obligations 4
personal philosophy 55
personal qualities 36, 71, 87
persuasiveness 40
PhD 21
Phi Beta Kappa 23
Poe, Edgar Allan 86
Point Scholarships 61
political interests 36
political issues 28
political magazines 26
politics 32
Ponsot, Marie 85, 87
practical problems 33
practicing 28
prizes 23
problem-solving 26
public policy 32
Public Policy and International Affairs Summer Institute 61
public service 28, 34, 35–6
purpose 4–5, 8, 9, 42, 60, 65, 75–6; articulation of 10–12, 31–2, 46–7; and "calling" 13; focus on 72; role of 12–13; statement of 24, 62; *see also* "Inventory of Purpose" exercise

"rambling" 84
"ranting" 84
reading 24, 26, 36
recognitions 6, 8, 14, 27, 36
recruitment strategies 108–9
referees 30–1
reflective practice 26
rejection, dealing with 22
relationships 6
religion 55; *see also* Islam
remote learning 111
research assistantships 28
residential counselling 28
resourcefulness 33

résumés 6, 29, 52, 78, 84, 97
revision 68, 95–8
Rhodes Scholarship 69, 78, 79, 95, 100
rock climbing 59

Sabin, Margaret xiv, xxi, 85, 93n1, 94n10
Samvid scholarship 31
satisfaction 32, 47
scholarship committees 22
scholarships: "building-block" 34; critical language" 34; definition 2–3, 16n7; internal 23; language 24, 100; merit-based 23, 34; need-based 34; purpose-driven 31–2; range of opportunities 3–4; and students from underrepresented backgrounds 61–2; successful applicants 19–37; as a way of life 9; *see also* fellowships
schooling 54
Schwarzman Scholarship 26, 28, 100
selection criteria 26, 62, 103
selection process 22
self, sense of 41, 43
self-betrayal 51
self-censoring 86
self-comprehension 44; *see also* self-understanding
self-confidence 33, 45, 49, 65
self-consciousness 86
self-cultivation 11–12, 101
self-defeating behaviors 45
self-discouragement 46–52
self-discovery 4
self-doubt 47, 50; *see also* imposter syndrome
self-knowledge 44
selflessness 76
self-narrative 70
self-presentation 42, 58–66, 71; *see also* authenticity
self-reliance 33
self-transcendence 50–1

self-transformation 11–12, 14
self-understanding 12, 41, 43–5, 47, 75
self-worth 4
seminars 25
Shagabayeva, Larisa 43
Shahawy, Hassaan 69, 74–80, 89
"showing up" 28
siblings 42, 53
Silicon Valley 49
skills: developing 35, 36, 112; "soft" 26, 28; writing 32–3
social background 48
social interests 36
social issues 28
social networks 7, 29
"soft skills" 26, 28
specialists 61
spirituality 55
sports team 26
storytelling 70–1
structure (in essay writing) 69–70
student governments 26–8, 35, 112
student loans 10
student organizations 26, 112–13
student publications 28
study abroad scholarships 23, 33–5, 110–11
subconscious factors 46
success 6, 8, 34; academic 25; "narratives" 45, 46, 52

teachers: cultivating relationships with 30; getting to know 24–6; language 34; learning from students 89–90; letters of recommendation from 30–1
teaching assistantships 28, 59
tenure 6, 110
theatre 28
touchstones 42–7

transformation 11
Truman Scholarship 26, 31
trust xix–xx, 21, 47, 50, 60, 114
"trusted reader" 99
Tsai, Alice 60
tuition 2
"turning points" 41, 42

Udall scholarship 31
Uddin, Maisha 64
unworthiness, feeling of 48, 50; *see also* imposter syndrome

value: of college degree 10; and self-transformation 11–12
vanity 14
viewpoints 33
vignettes 61, 69
virtue-signalling 77
volunteering 28
"vomit draft" 85

Weber, Max 12
What You're Really Meant to Do 45
When There Are Nine Scholarship 61
word count 98–9
work lives 43
workshops 113
writing: courses 32; "Dear Mother" tactic 86; developing skills 32–3; exercises 40–1, 85, 90; fast 84; removing mental and emotional roadblocks 86; stories of one's own life 44–5; *see also* application essays; drafts; revision; word count

yearbooks 26
"Youth Purpose Study" questionnaire 14; *see also* "Inventory of Purpose" exercise